LEICESTERSH
RUTLAND TALES OF
MYSTERY AND
MURDER

LEICESTERSHIRE & RUTLAND TALES OF MYSTERY AND MURDER

David Bell

COUNTRYSIDE BOOKS
Newbury, Berkshire

First published 2002
© David Bell 2002

COUNTRYSIDE BOOKS
3 Catherine Road
Newbury, Berkshire

To view our complete range of books,
please visit us at
www.countrysidebooks.co.uk

ISBN 1 85306 758 X

For Rosemary

Produced through MRM Associates Ltd., Reading
Typeset by Mac Style Ltd, Scarborough, N. Yorkshire
Printed by J. W. Arrowsmith Ltd., Bristol

Contents

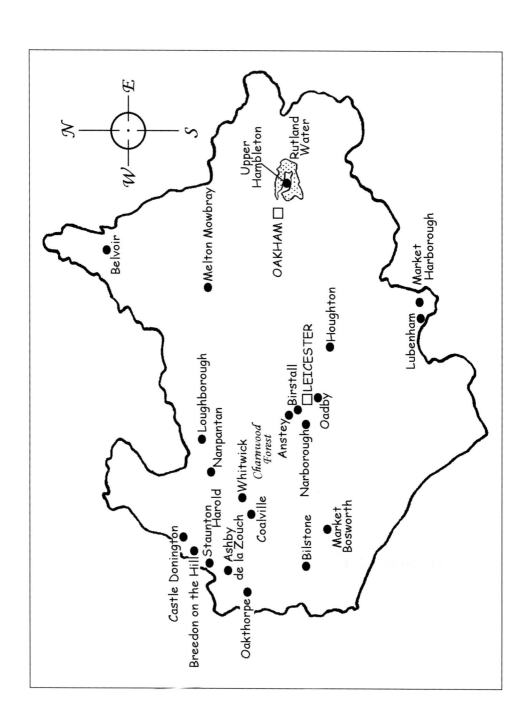

INTRODUCTION

The tales of mystery and murder contained in this book range through Leicestershire and Rutland's history as well as events from the late 20th century. It begins with the account of what happened to the three female members of the Flower family accused of murdering the sons of the Earl of Rutland 'by wicked practice and sorcery' during the reign of James I. Also here is another of Leicestershire's witches – Black Annis – who started her life as a benevolent pre-Christian goddess but now has a reputation as a child-eating fiend. The fierce and lecherous Red Comyn of Whitwick Castle makes an appearance, as do two 'rarities of nature' in the form of the 53 stone Daniel Lambert and the tiny Captain Jeffrey Hudson.

Another surprising character in the book is Richard III, regarded in Leicestershire as a gallant and noble king, yet portrayed by William Shakespeare as a crookbacked villain who murdered his nephews.

Among the murderers are a local aristocrat who was hanged in 1760 and a local wrestler hanged in 1801. There are 20th century murder cases too, including an examination of just who did kill Bella Wright in the notorious green bicycle murder of 1919, the case of the Rutland 'Walter Mitty' who killed both of his parents in 1993, the case of the first use of DNA fingerprinting in 1987, and a case that – rightly or wrongly – became known as the 'Hot Dog Wars'.

There is also a visit to Ned Ludd, the Anstey man who inadvertently gave a new word to the English language, an investigation of the wild big cats that roam the countryside in Rutland and Leicestershire, and an account of Papillon Hall, once Leicestershire's most haunted building.

In fact, a mix of stories that I hope will inform and entertain you.

Happy reading!

David Bell

THE WITCHES OF BELVOIR CASTLE

Witches have been ill-treated by the authorities – including the church – during much of this country's history. They have been harassed, arrested, tortured, and sentenced to death. Despite the myths and several historically inaccurate films, witches in England were executed by hanging, with burning at the stake being reserved for heretics.

One of the monarchs who was particularly harsh on witches was James I. The Elizabethan age had been fairly moderate in its attitudes to witchcraft, the queen refusing to condemn alleged witches to death. However, when James VI of Scotland succeeded to the English throne, he turned the clock back in that respect. He even wrote a book called *Daemonologie*, urging his subjects to seek out witches and bring them to trial.

Who were these witches? It is sometimes argued that they were a surviving remnant of older pre-Christian religion but I think the vast majority of them must have been women who lived alone. If they had some knowledge of the medical properties of herbs and plants, this made them suspect in an atmosphere in which the official church attitude to illness was that it was sent from God. Attempting to cure it was obviously flying against the will of the Almighty. It followed that the knowledge of the curative effect of herbs could not come from God and so it must come from his arch-enemy Satan. If these wise women also kept a pet – a cat or a tame raven, for example – and even spoke to the animal, this was additional evidence that they were witches. They were communicating with the Devil by means of his messengers, who came disguised as animals. If any old women suffered from hallucinations, or talked to themselves, or were simply old or ugly, or behaved in a strange manner, they were in imminent danger of being regarded as witches.

It was in this superstitious atmosphere that Francis, the sixth Earl of Rutland, from Belvoir Castle in Leicestershire, suffered a double bereavement. His young son, Henry, Lord Rosse, became seriously ill and died. This tragic event was soon followed by the sickness and slow death of the earl's younger son, Francis, and the illness of his daughter Katherine. The grief-stricken earl and his wife Cecilia thought about the situation. Such events could surely not come from God; so the obvious answer was that they had been caused by witchcraft. In December 1617, he had six local women arrested and charged.

The six women were Joan Flower of Langham, her daughters Margaret and Phillipa (written as Phillip in contemporary documents), Anne Baker of Bottesford, Joan Willimot of Goadby and Ellen Greene of Stathern. Joan Flower had been reputed to be a witch for years. The evidence included the fact that she was extremely ugly, often swore in a harsh voice, and never went to church. Her daughter Phillipa had been accused of witchcraft on completely different grounds by a local man, Thomas Simpson. His account – a man's excuse, if ever I heard one – was that Phillipa had bewitched him into falling in love with her to such a degree that he couldn't control his mind or his body! I think it is safe to assume that Phillipa was prettier than her mother.

Joan's other daughter, Margaret, had been employed at Belvoir Castle as a poultrymaid and laundrymaid, but had been dismissed for stealing food. Perhaps the earl's servants were not too well fed! When the earl was casting around for someone to blame for the death of his children (today he might have considered suing a hospital or a doctor), he must have remembered the sacking of Margaret Flower.

What happened to the six women in the days and weeks that followed can only be imagined. They were obviously closely questioned, and probably tortured. Certainly by the time they were brought before the judges of the assizes in February and March, all six were ready to make confessions.

Phillipa Flower confessed that an evil spirit came to her in the form of a white rat, and that she allowed it to suck from her left breast. In return, the spirit had enabled her to make Thomas Simpson fall in love with her.

Margaret Flower confessed that she had often entertained two familiar spirits, one white and one black, which she had allowed to suck from her and she had promised them her soul. She said that since her arrest she had also been visited in prison by four devils: one a black-headed ape, which spoke to her in a tongue she couldn't understand, and another Rutterkin, her mother's cat. The other two visiting devils she called Little Robin and Spirit. Margaret also confessed that four years earlier her mother had instructed her to steal a glove belonging to Henry, Lord Rosse, the elder son of her employer. Her mother had boiled the glove, pricked it through many times with a knife and rubbed it on her cat Rutterkin, before burning it. She confessed that she had later found a glove belonging to Henry's brother, Francis. It too had been put into hot water and rubbed on Rutterkin's back, but this glove was buried in a dungheap to rot. Margaret said that her mother had commanded her to bring home a handkerchief of Lady Katherine, the earl's daughter. This too was put into hot water and rubbed on the belly of the cat. However, on this occasion the cat whined, and had no power to hurt the girl.

The implication of this confession was not lost on the public. The burnt glove had caused Henry, Lord Rosse to die, while his brother Francis had sickened and died as the

THE
WONDERFVL
DISCOVERIE OF THE
Witchcrafts of *Margaret* and *Phillip*
Flower, daughters of *Joan Flower* neere *Beuer Castle*: executed at Lincolne, *March* 11. 1618.

Who were specially arraigned & condemned before
Sir *Henry Hobart*, and Sir *Edward Bromley*, Judges of Assize, for confessing themselues actors in the destruction of *Henry*, Lord *Rosse*, with their damnable practises against others the Children of the Right Honourable FRANCIS Earle of *Rutland*.

Together with the seuerall Examinations and Confessions of *Anne Baker*, *Ioan Willimot*, and *Ellen Greene*, Witches in *Leicestershire*.

Printed at London by *G. Eld* for *I. Barnes*, dwelling in the long Walke neere Christ-Church. 1619.

The front cover of a pamphlet detailing the trial of the Belvoir witches. It was published in 1619 and shows Anne Baker, Joan Willimot and Ellen Greene.

second glove had rotted in the dungheap. The spell on Katherine had not worked and thus she recovered from her sickness.

Margaret Flower also said that she and her mother had used other spells – including mixing some wool from the countess's mattress with warm water and blood – to prevent the earl and countess from having more children. Not only were the accused women guilty of witchcraft, they were using it to interfere with the earl's line of succession. This was treason as well as devilry.

The accounts of the confessions of the other three accused women reveal that Anne Baker suffered from visual and aural hallucinations. She talked of seeing four planets in the sky: one black, one yellow, one green and one blue. She said that the appearance of the black planet always foretold death. In a rambling manner she told how she had seen the blue planet strike the head of Thomas Fairebarne but that he had recovered. She also told of seeing both a flash of fire and a hand in the sky and hearing a voice which warned her of danger. Anne was charged with causing the death of a child that had been brought to her for help, and also the death of Elizabeth Hough in a quarrel over the quality of some bread. She denied both accusations. It does seem possible that Anne Baker – known to see strange visions and hear voices – was thought locally to possess special powers. People would bring a sick child to her to be cured, and when she failed she might easily be suspected of having caused the death, in a muddled confusion between having killed and having failed to cure. Also, following any petty dispute, Anne Baker might well have been thought to have sought revenge through her alleged powers. Anne did give some evidence in the case of the deaths of the earl's sons, saying that three years earlier she had been told by two local women that the death of Henry, Lord Rosse had been caused by the burying of a glove, causing his liver to rot. This account seems to mix up the glove belonging to Henry,

The Rutland monument at St Mary's church, Bottesford.

said by Margaret Flower to have been burnt, and the glove belonging to Francis, which was buried.

The public examinations of Joan Willimot and Ellen Greene brought about the naming of other so-called witches, interestingly male: Gamaliel Greete of Waltham and William Berry of Langham. Ellen seems to have been the more forthcoming (more vindictive?) of the two, accusing Joan of having two familiar spirits, one a kitten and one a moldiwarp (a local term for a mole). The kitten, called Pusse, was said to feed from Joan's neck below her right ear, while the moldiwarp, called Hiffe Hiffe, fed from the corresponding place below her left ear. Ellen accused Joan Willimot of sending her familiars to cause the death of a woman and her newly born child in Stathern. The evidence of these two women is an example of how accused witches were urged to inform on one another and give the authorities further names to investigate. Both women gave evidence that Joan Flower had familiars and that she had used spells to harm the earl's family.

The fate of Anne Baker, Joan Willimot and Ellen Greene is not known. It seems possible that their punishment was less than that of the three women of the Flower family. Joan Flower died in Lincoln prison while eating a piece of bread. The prison authorities issued a statement alleging that before she ate it she said, 'If I am guilty of any witchcraft, may I be struck dead on the spot.' Then she proceeded to choke to death. Here was proof indeed that she must be guilty. Her two daughters, Margaret and Phillipa, were therefore guilty by association, and were hanged on the gallows.

A year after the trials of the Belvoir witches, a pamphlet about the case was published in London. The cover of the pamphlet bore a drawing of Anne Baker, Joan Willimot and Ellen Greene, and the confessions of the six women were detailed.

An even more permanent reminder of the events can be

found in St Mary's church in Bottesford. On the monument of Francis, the sixth Earl of Rutland, the following words are recorded: 'In 1605 He Married Ye Lady Cecelia Hungerford Daughter To Ye Honble Knight Sir John Tufton By Whom He Had Two Sons Both Wch Died In Their Infancy By Wicked Practice and Sorcerye'. This makes Bottesford church unique, because it is the only English church to contain within its walls a reference to the topic of witchcraft ('wicked practice') and sorcery.

But one mystery remains. Were the accused women really malicious witches with genuine powers? Certainly the Earl of Rutland thought so. Were they just foolish women who believed they had evil powers and wished to harm the family of the Earl of Rutland, using their reputations to impress their neighbours? Or were they simply local women who got caught up in the superstitious atmosphere of the early 17th century, cruelly killed by a Leicestershire nobleman who was overwhelmed by grief and looking for someone to blame for the death of his sons? We can only guess.

THE HOT DOG WARS

The case that came to be known as the Leicester Hot Dog Wars began in the early hours of Tuesday, 28 August 1990. It was the night following the bank holiday Monday. Gary Thompson and his friend and employee John Derek Weston had spent the late evening counting the weekend's takings from their fast food outlets at the Abbey Park Show and Leicester Air Show. They brought the money back to their depot in Aylestone Road and then set off for Gary's luxury home in Oadby. They had a large sum of money – later estimated to be between £28,000 and £60,000 – with them.

Who were the two men? Gary Thompson, originally from Great Glen, was generally acknowledged to be Leicester's hot dog king. He was 32 years old, and married with an 11 year old daughter and an 8 year old son. He was a wealthy man. Three years earlier he had been jailed for 21 months for evading VAT amounting to £411,000. At that time he was declaring a taxable income of £25,000 per annum, although he was described in court as a fast-food businessman with an estimated income of £3 million over six years. He owned a Rolls Royce with personalized number plates and a Range Rover, as well as 21 vehicles connected with his business. He was also a big man, heavily built and weighing 25 stones. His friend John Weston, commonly known by his second name Derek, was 29, and originally from Stoke-on-Trent. Derek had left his girlfriend and 3 year old son, and was now living with a 16 year old girl at Gary Thompson's house.

As Gary and Derek drove back to Oadby at 2 am with their bank holiday takings in Gary's car, now a Bentley, they were being followed by another car, a silver Ford Sierra. As the Bentley pulled into Thompson's drive and the two men got out, the Sierra pulled in behind them. Two masked men got out, one of them carrying a Beretta pistol, and, minutes later, five shots rang out. The men got back into their Sierra, which reversed at speed from the drive, and then sped off along the A6. Gary Thompson lay dead on his lawn, shot in the legs, stomach and head; Derek Weston lay dying on the drive, shot in the legs and head.

Five days later, the burnt out Sierra was spotted by a lorry driver at Beeby, about 8 miles from the scene of the shooting. The police quickly discovered that it had been taken on the bank holiday Monday from outside the Scraptoft Valley Working Men's Club on the Netherhall estate. It had been abandoned and burnt about a mile from where it had been stolen. The police thought that after the killings it had probably been driven via Stoughton and Thurnby, to avoid the city. They also thought it might have tailed Gary Thompson from his depot in Aylestone Road. They appealed for information from anyone who might have seen the car, with its distinctive KERNOW (Cornish for Cornwall) sticker, on its final journey.

An incident room was set up at Wigston, with Detective Superintendent Graham Blandford in charge of a team of 40 officers. Derek Weston's girlfriend described how she had opened the door to investigate the skirmish taking place on the drive, but closed it again when she heard the shots. Mavis Thompson said that she had run out of the house towards the struggle, until her husband ordered her back in.

From the very beginning, the possibility was raised that the killings were the result of a business dispute between rivals over fast food pitches, and the phrase 'The Hot Dog Wars' was coined. It was obvious that there had been an intent to kill; both men had been shot in the head. However, Edgar Thompson, Gary's father, who said that his son was very generous and extremely popular, did not accept this

LEICESTERSHIRE CONSTABULARY

DOUBLE MURDER AT OADBY

These two men were shot dead outside their home on the main A6 road, Oadby at 2 am, Tuesday 28th August, 1990, which followed the August Bank Holiday Monday

GARY THOMPSON　　　　**JOHN WESTON**

This metallic silver Sierra car was stolen between 8.30 pm and 10.35 pm on Bank Holiday Monday near to Scraptoft Valley WMC, Grantham Rd, Netherhall.

The vehicle is connected with the murder and was found burnt out in a field near Beeby off the Scraptoft Lane, opposite its junction with Keyham Lane, the following morning.

DID YOU SEE THIS CAR?
HAVE YOU ANY INFORMATION REGARDING THE PERSONS RESPONSIBLE?

If so, then ring in confidence the Incident Room.
Leicester 485455

£100,000 REWARD

A reward of £100,000 has been offered for information leading to the arrest and conviction of the person or persons responsible.

Printed and Published by the Chief Constable, Leicestershire Constabulary

A police appeal for information issued in connection with the murder of hot dog king Gary Thompson and his associate John Derek Weston.

scenario. Edgar put up a reward of £100,000 – the largest reward ever offered by an individual – for information leading to an arrest.

The police announced that they were looking for two white men: one of them muscular and 6 feet tall, the other a few inches shorter and slimmer. Graham Blandford said that he thought they were local men who knew about the victims' money and movements. He thought that the gunman may have been holding Gary Thompson at gunpoint while his accomplice tried to wrestle the money from Derek Weston. He added that the heavily built Thompson would have been unlikely to give up the money easily.

On 11 September, it seemed that a result was in the offing when over 20 police officers, 10 of them armed, raided a converted barn in King's Cliffe at 6.25 am. Two men were arrested. However, this proved to be a red herring, which was explained when a publican from Stamford was fined £400 for giving false information; suspicious about the two co-owners of his pub, he had made an anonymous call to the police naming them as the killers.

It was five weeks later that two men were arrested and charged with the murder of Gary Thompson and Derek Weston; they were Warren Slaney of Tyrell Street, Leicester, and Terrence Burke from the Netherhall estate. A third man, Andrew Robinson, was charged with conspiracy to rob. The trial of Slaney and Burke took place in February 1992 before Mr Justice Owen and a jury of five men and seven women. Everyone attending the trial had to pass through a metal detector, and the two defendants sat in the dock behind a bullet-proof glass screen.

The prosecution case was that Robinson and Burke knew each other from their work as bouncers at a pub in the Haymarket, and they both knew Slaney, who was a former professional boxer. The prosecution alleged that the original plan was for Andrew Robinson to drive Slaney and Burke to

Gary Thompson's depot in Aylestone Road. There the two men were to shoot the Rottweiller guard dog and steal the weekend's takings. However, when they arrived at the depot, there were too many people there, and Thompson's Bentley was parked in such a way as to make the raid impossible. Leaving Robinson in his car, Slaney and Burke followed Gary Thompson to his Oadby home in another car, stolen earlier that day. During the robbery outside Thompson's house, the prosecution claimed, Warren Slaney shot the two men. Eventually, Robinson, still waiting near the depot, received a mobile phone call telling him to go home. Later Burke and Robinson met Slaney at a lock-up garage, where two heavy holdalls containing the money were loaded into the boot of a car borrowed from Burke's sister. The pistol was thrown into a gravel pit at Wanlip, and was later recovered by the police.

Terrence Burke admitted that he and Warren Slaney had been partners in the projected robbery and that he had grappled with Gary Thompson at the scene of the crime. He insisted that he had thought that the reason for taking a pistol was to get rid of the dog at the depot, and that he was shocked when it was used to shoot the men. When Andrew Robinson was told of the shooting, he asked Slaney why he had used the gun, and received the calm reply, 'Slimline got out of hand.' He understood the nickname 'Slimline' to refer to Gary Thompson.

Andrew Robinson told the court that he had already pleaded guilty in another court to conspiracy with Burke and Slaney to rob Gary Thompson, and was awaiting sentence. (He was later given four years in prison.) He had received £1,000 for his part in the night's activities. His girlfriend told the court that she had seen Burke and Slaney trying on balaclava masks in the street, just hours before the raid. She said that Warren Slaney was singing at the time. The three men then drove off. She also said, although Burke never mentioned the crime, Slaney had later spoken of how he'd enjoyed shooting the victims, adding that he was spending the money on dining out and drinking champagne.

The police said that they had recovered £4,000 in four envelopes and £615 in cash from Burke's home, and an envelope containing £675 at Slaney's house.

Expert witnesses gave evidence that the Beretta pistol was fired only 18 inches from Thompson's head and could not have been fired accidentally. It was also found to have an adaptor for a silencer attached to it. The killing was deliberate, as the victims had been first disabled with shots to the legs and body.

In his evidence Terrence Burke told of three men who had recruited him to commit the robbery, telling him that it was an insurance scam set up by Gary Thompson. They were to steal the money, which would be about £25,000; then Thompson would claim £60,000, plus the value of some jewellery, from his insurance company. He had believed the story right until the moment when Gary Thompson had put up a struggle while being robbed. He had believed that Slaney knew the raid was a mock one, and was shocked when Slaney shot the two men. He told the court that he was too scared to name the three organizers. Burke also said that, while on remand, Slaney had warned him to keep quiet about what he knew, threatening him with half a pair of scissors. When the incident had been reported to the prison governor, Slaney had been moved to another prison.

Warren Slaney's barrister stated that his client denied being present at any of the events of that night, and that Burke and Robinson had conspired to blame him. Although Slaney had opted not to give evidence himself, nine witnesses claimed that they were with him on the night of the shootings. Slaney's aunt said that he had been at a party at her house on the Monday night, talking and watching television, and had not left until 4.30 am. His cousins Carol and Alan confirmed this, and six other people gave evidence that they were present and had seen him that night. Carol

Free Warren Slaney

On the 10th of Oct. 1990 Warren Slaney was arrested and later charged with the murder of 2 men, Gary Thompson and John Weston, in Oadby, Leicester.

The murders took place at 2am outside the house of Gary & Mavis Thompson. The police suggested that 3 men were directly involved in an armed "robbery" that backfired.

As a result Warren Slaney is now serving life imprisonment for a crime he did not commit.

INNOCENT

- **Physical descriptions** given by eye witnesses do not match Warren Slaney's appearance
  Witness 1 :- that the perpetrators were over 6ft and of the same build as Gary Thompson (about 21st).
  Witness 2 :- that one was 6ft-6ft 1", broad, heavily built, dark tan, big moustache, hat with pony tail.

  Warren Slaney is 5ft 8" white, clean shaven and had very short hair. At the time he weighed between 9½-10st.

- **9 witnesses** were with Warren at a party till 4.30am on the morning of the murders.
- **A crucial prosecution witness** testified in court that she had falsified her statement to the police. This statement implicated Warren Slaney directly in the "robbery".
- The man who disposed of the gun admitted that Warren had nothing to do with the murders. This statement was not used in court.
- Warren was accused of firing the Berretta handgun which killed 2 men. The shots fired displayed a great degree of accuracy. Warren had previously suffered hand injuries which resulted in the insertion of metal plates. He would not have been capable of such an act because he would not have been capable of pulling the trigger. This medical evidence was never used by the defence.
- **there was no forensic evidence** to link Warren to the murders although the police searched his home 4 times.

THE TRIAL

Crucial evidence relating to Warren's innocence was not brought up in court by the defence. His solicitor briefed a QC only 2 weeks before the trial. Leaving inadequate time for Warren's defence.

- 8 days of the trial were spent on 3 prosecution witnesses and only 3 hours on the 9 defence witnesses.
- As Paddy Hill said on the release of the 'Bridgewater 4' "...they get a suspect, and what they do is they try to fit the circumstances and evidence of the crime around the suspect.....Every time they do that that is a recipe for disaster."

A publicity handout from the 'Free Warren Slaney' campaign.

Kirk denied that she had persuaded the other witnesses that they had seen Warren Slaney at the bank holiday party, and not at her engagement party two days earlier.

After the judge had summed up, describing the events in the suburb of Oadby as 'like a Chicago film', the jury retired. They brought in a verdict of guilty, and Warren Slaney and Terrence Burke each received two life sentences for murder, and 16 years for conspiracy to rob. As he was led away, Slaney spoke for the first time, shouting, 'Innocent man. I hope you remember!' He removed his tie and held it up like a noose towards the jury, adding, 'I have been framed. I am an innocent man.'

Burke's family accepted the verdict, his father saying, 'He did what he did and got what he deserved.' However, Slaney's family and friends continued to protest his innocence and to campaign for his release. His cousin Carol said, 'He was unable to speak in court on the advice of his lawyer. We will speak for him.' Demonstrations were held outside his prison and outside the Home Office. Three groups – Liberty, Conviction and, perhaps more surprisingly, The National Association of Probation Officers – supported the call for Warren Slaney's conviction to be re-investigated, on the grounds that it might be unsafe or unsatisfactory. This appeal was turned down in 1992. Four years later, Slaney again tried to get leave to challenge his conviction on the grounds that he had been inadequately represented in court and should have been strongly advised to give evidence on his own behalf, but again the appeal failed. His friends and family have never accepted the verdict, and the support group held a 50-mile cycle ride to draw attention to the campaign in May 2000.

What really did happen that night – and why it happened – remains a mystery. Gary Thompson's family firmly believes that both men were brutally murdered for monetary gain. Detective Superintendent Blandford adds that he always said it was a robbery that went wrong. But the doubts remain.

There had been extreme rivalry between the various men operating the hot dog concessions in Leicester for many years. In 1978, Gary Thompson, then aged 20, was fined £4,000 for paying two men to raid the premises of a rival, Geno Loizzo. They stole a freezer, hot dog stalls and signs, 300 burgers and 1,000 bread rolls. Thompson was also found guilty of attacking one of Loizzo's employees, named Persico.

In March 1991, seven months after the shootings, Joe Persico, described in the *Leicester Mercury* as a self-styled street fighter who had served four years for grievous bodily harm, went into hiding after his family received the body of a pig with its eyelids cut off. A scar and receding hair had been drawn on the pig's head to make it resemble him, and he stated that he understood there was a £25,000 contract on his life. In the days that followed, Persico's father had his house windows blasted with a shotgun, and his cousin in Derby had his garage showroom windows shattered. Persico believed he was being blamed for helping the police with their inquiry into the Oadby shootings. In October 1991, Joe Persico distributed hundreds of leaflets, accusing an ex-proprietor of a Leicester security firm of being involved in the shooting of Gary Thompson.

In the same year, Roger Cook, the television investigator, came to Leicester to film what was going on between the various hot dog kings. He set a hot dog van in the street and posed as a salesman. After only a few minutes he was assaulted, and his van was hitched up to a vehicle and driven away. The film, broadcast on Central ITV, showed that the man towing away the van was Joe Persico.

There are many questions about this murder that remain unanswered. There is the question of who at the trial was telling the truth. Were there three underworld chiefs who hired Terrence Burke? Did he really think that the robbery was an insurance swindle? Why were Gary Thompson and his partner executed by being shot in the head in what looked like a gangster-style killing? Was Warren Slaney the man who committed the shootings, or were the nine people who gave him an alibi for that night correct about the date? And if Warren Slaney wasn't the man, who was there in Oadby with Terrence Burke to pull the trigger?

GODDESS OR WITCH?

In Leicester, one of the threats made by mothers to persuade their children to go to sleep goes, 'If you kids ain't asleep in five minutes, Black Annis'll come and eat yer!' Whether this gruesome statement actually induces calm sleep or a terrified nightmare is a moot point, but the more interesting question is who Black Annis was (or is still). According to legend, she was a witch who lived in a wild area to the west of Leicester called Dane Hills. Although Leicester people have always called her a witch, she must have been something immortal, since she was around in pagan times, in the Middle Ages, in the 18th century, and – according to some – is still here today.

However, Robert Graves describes the original Annis as a beautiful goddess, worshipped locally in pre-Christian times. She was also called Anna, Anu or Danu; and Dane Hills – far from being a reference to the Vikings, as might easily be assumed – were in fact called Danu's Hills, and the area was a sacred one. Annis took great interest in the crops, and was regarded as entirely benevolent. The pagan people loved and respected her, and she gave them plentiful harvests in return.

When Christianity came to England, the authorities were not willing to have any rival deities; the priests denounced Annis as an evil creature, and down the centuries it is this version of the Annis legend that has survived. According to Leicester folklore, Annis had one eye, a blue face and long, sharp pointed teeth. Her hands were actually sharp talons, as hard as iron, which she used to kill her victims. She lived in a cave, 8 feet wide and 5 feet tall, known as Black Annis's Bower. People said that Annis had dug out the cave herself with those powerful talons. Not far from the cave was a large oak tree, the last remnant of an ancient forest, and Annis would hide in its branches, dropping down onto passers-by, before killing and eating them. She hung the skins of her victims on the walls of the cave and used them to make her clothing.

John Heyrick, who combined writing poetry with a career as a soldier, lived in Leicestershire in the second half of the 18th century. On the subject of Dane Hills, he wrote:

Where down the plain the winding pathway falls
From Glenfield village to Leicester's ancient walls;
Nature or art with imitative power
Far in the glen has placed Black Annis's Bower.
'Tis said the soul of mortal man recoiled
To view Black Annis's eye so fierce and wild.
Vast talons, foul with human flesh, there grew
In place of hands, and features vivid blue
Glared in her visage; whilst her obscene waist
Warm skins of human victims embraced.

When Annis failed to find humans for her dinner, she would hunt and eat wild animals, particularly hares. She could outrun the hares, and ate them raw as soon as she caught them. Up until the 18th century, the Mayor of Leicester, together with many other local worthies, would attend an annual fair on Dane Hills on Easter Monday. At midday, he would take part in hunting a hare and it seems highly likely that the killing of the hare was some kind of echo of an animal sacrifice to Black Annis. In later years, the hunting of a live hare was abandoned. It was replaced with a drag hunt, the dogs following the trail of a dead cat soaked in aniseed and tied to the tail of a horse, though this practice might seem equally gruesome to us today.

Interestingly, the name Cat Anna is sometimes used in Leicester to describe a gossipy or unpleasant neighbour.

Annis crops up in another local legend. In 1485, King Richard III was riding west from Leicester at the head of his army to engage in battle with Henry Tudor. As he crossed Bow Bridge, his heel struck the parapet, and Annis appeared in the crowd, shrieking out, 'Your heel has hit it on the way out, and your head will hit it on the way back in.' What the king made of this weird prophecy is not recorded, but when the two armies met at the Battle of Bosworth, Richard was killed. His corpse was thrown ignominiously onto a horse and brought back to Leicester. Just as Black Annis had foretold, as his body was brought across Bow Bridge, the head struck the parapet.

In Victorian times, when melodramas were in vogue, there were several plays written about Black Annis. One was entitled *Black Anna's Bower or the Maniac of the Dane Hills*, and Annis is of course the villainous maniac of the title. In the play called *The Broken Heart*, however, Annis is a wronged woman driven insane after the murder of her husband and baby; so here at least the evil version of Annis has been amended.

Two recent fantasy novels feature Black Annis. She appears in Graham Joyce's *Dark Sister*, and in Freda Warrington's *The Rainbow Gate*, though in the latter Annis has been transported from Dane Hills to Bradgate Park. I can understand why; Dane Hills is now covered in modern housing, whereas Bradgate remains wild, rocky and mysterious. In *The Rainbow Gate*, Annis is once again an evil creature, but in *Dark Sister* the balance between malevolence and benevolence is much more ambivalent.

For many centuries no one wanted to live in Dane Hills, because of the scary reputation of Black Annis, and so it was the late 1940s before houses were actually built there. On the spot where the notorious cave had been, the convent of St Catherine now stands. Surely that ought to keep the witch down! Mind you, there is a story that a tunnel led from the back of the cave all the way to Leicester Castle. That is some tunnel, especially if it was dug using only talons. But there are accounts of Black Annis now appearing at the castle's Rupert's Gate. It is said that even the streetwise scared-of-nothing Leicester kids of today will not go there after dark, as – once again – the whisper is out: 'Black Annis will catch you and eat you!'

The children who half-believe this are part of a long tradition of Leicester people who accepted the version of Annis spread by the early church when they were attempting to replace pagan beliefs with Christianity. Others try to reclaim her earlier reputation as a powerful but benevolent goddess, and a few years ago there was a women's garland dancing troupe that proudly bore the name of Black Annis.

Rupert's Gate at Leicester Castle, said to be haunted still by Black Annis.

Strangely, when I went to Leicester Castle in May 2002 to photograph Rupert's Gate, only the photographs taken from outside the gate came out well. Every picture taken from inside the gate was ruined by a large black oval shape, although all the photos taken before and after on the same film came out normally. Could Black Annis be trying to tell me something?

WHO KILLED BELLA WRIGHT?

The case of Bella Wright, murdered in 1919, has never reached a conclusion, although in June 1920 it seemed that everything was cut and dried. Her murderer had been caught and was on trial. The prosecution was being led by the attorney general, and it seemed that the evidence was overwhelming.

Annie Bella Wright was nine days short of her 22nd birthday when she was killed. She lived with her parents in the village of Stoughton, a rural spot only 3 miles east of Leicester. Bella worked at Bates' Rubber Mill in Leicester, making pneumatic bike tyres. Her colleagues at work included her friend Sally Ward, whose younger brother, Archie, was a stoker in the navy. Although Archie was only 17, he and Bella were walking out. They weren't officially engaged, but it was generally accepted that they would one day get married.

One of the perks of working at the rubber factory was that employees could buy bicycle tyres at a discount, and Bella was a regular cyclist. One Saturday evening in July 1919, after biking over into Evington to post a letter to Archie, Bella decided to cycle the 5 miles over to Gaulby to visit her Uncle George. On the way she had some trouble with her bike chain, but while she was struggling with it, a passing cyclist, a well-spoken man in his mid-thirties, stopped and helped her, and then cycled alongside her as far as Gaulby. When Bella went to her Uncle George's cottage, the man cycled away.

Bella Wright, shot as she rode her bicycle along the Via Devana.

Bella spent a very enjoyable time there with her Uncle George, a local character with a bushy beard and a wooden peg leg. Bella was delighted that her cousin Margaret from Yorkshire was there with her husband James and their new baby. When George went to the door at one point he noticed a man with a green BSA bicycle lurking about. He didn't like the look of him, and pointed him out to Bella. She didn't seem concerned, and said it was the man she'd met earlier. She added that if he was still around when it was time for her to leave, she would try to give him the slip. She stayed for almost two hours, admiring the baby and talking about bicycles with James, himself a cycling enthusiast. It was about nine o'clock before Bella decided to set out for home.

When Bella's relatives came to the door to wave her goodbye they were disconcerted to see the man with the bicycle still hanging around. He called out to Bella, 'I thought you'd gone the other way home,' and Uncle George was sure the man had used Bella's name. However, Bella still did not seem worried and set off for Stoughton, dismissing her family's fears. Once she had gone, James wished that he had volunteered to accompany her home, and Uncle George wished he had seen the stranger off earlier in the evening.

They were right to be concerned: Bella Wright was never seen alive again. Her dead body was discovered 20 minutes later, by local farmer Joe Cowell as he walked along the Gartree Road, known locally as the Via Devana. She was lying in a pool of blood, half on the road, half on the grass verge. As Joe Cowell lifted Bella onto the grass, he realized that although she was still warm there were no signs of life. He propped her bicycle against a nearby field gate before returning to his farm. He sent two farmhands to guard the body, while he set off on horseback to summon help.

It was 10.30 pm and getting dark when PC Alf Hall arrived. With the aid of the two workers, he lifted the bicycle and the body onto the back of a horse-drawn milk cart. At this point, a local doctor, Dr Kynaston Williams, arrived by car. He examined the body and told the young police constable that Bella had died from loss of blood following a sudden haemorrhage, or from exhaustion from her cycling. It is possible that the medical man did not approve of such unfeminine activities. Bella's body was taken to a disused chapel at nearby Little Stretton, where Dr Williams made a second examination, this time by candlelight, but found nothing new.

The story might have ended there, except for the initiative shown by the young police constable. Dissatisfied with the doctor's version of the likely events, and puzzled why there was no blood on Bella's coat or on her bicycle, Alf Hall returned to the chapel next morning. He checked the bicycle and confirmed that, apart from a little blood on one pedal, there was none on the rest of the bike. He also examined the body, and in the centre of some facial bruising he found a small hole, possibly caused by a bullet. After informing his superiors, Alf Hall returned to the spot where Bella's body had been found the previous night.

There he discovered the macabre sight of a dead bird, a crow or a raven, which appeared to have gorged itself to death on the blood in the road. There was blood on the field gate, and a man-made track leading into the field from the spot where Bella had been killed. The fact that the Via Devana had been reopened to traffic, plus the overnight rain, did not help his investigation, but with the aid of Joe Cowell he made a detailed search of the area. Eventually at 3 pm he found a spent bullet, trampled into the rough surface of the road by the feet of passing cattle. The bullet was a .455 and had marks on it suggesting that it had been fired from a revolver.

After reporting his finds to his sergeant, PC Hall went to see Dr Williams and suggested that he re-examine the girl's body. The medical man was obviously irritated by this intervention by a rural constable and said that he might call in at the chapel on the Monday, if he happened to be in the area. Unperturbed, the young police officer said that he was not satisfied and would have to call in a different doctor. Dr Williams rapidly changed his mind and was at Little Stretton within the hour. He now agreed that a bullet might have caused the hole in the face. Removing Bella's hat – surprisingly he had not removed it during his initial examinations of the body – the doctor discovered what looked like a bullet's exit wound. Later the post mortem confirmed that Bella had indeed been shot, and the coroner's inquest brought in a verdict of 'wilful murder by some person unknown'.

The police investigation began, and it was of course based on the search for the stranger on the green bicycle. A handbill was circulated, detailing the description of the man

The green bicycle retrieved from the Grand Union canal is carried into court at Leicester. (Leicestershire Constabulary)

and his cycle. The press – local newspapers at first but rapidly spreading to the nationals – took up the story. In some versions the account told of a young woman fleeing from a madman wielding a revolver as he pursued her on his green bicycle. After reading these sensational reports, a man living in his mother's house in the Highfields area of Leicester dismantled his green cycle, filed off its serial number, and dumped it in the Grand Union canal. He also threw in a holster for a revolver and a number of bullets. He may well have thrown in a revolver too.

It was in February 1920, seven months later, that a piece of this cycle was discovered when it snagged on the towrope of a horse-drawn coal barge. Although the bike frame fell back into the canal, the barge owner, Enoch Whitehouse, had noted that it was green. He returned to the spot the next day with a boat hook and managed to fish out the front wheel and frame of a bicycle. He called out excitedly to a man on the towpath. There were two amazing coincidences in this part of the story: the barge was delivering coal to the Bates Rubber factory, where Bella had worked, and the man on the towpath was the father of Archie Ward, Bella's sailor sweetheart!

The police engaged in a three week search of the canal, watched by an enthusiastic crowd of Leicester citizens, who cheered loudly every time a piece of debris was pulled out. More of the cycle was recovered, along with the gun holster and some ammunition, though the revolver itself was never found. The police called in the local BSA agent to examine the bicycle, and he found that, although the serial number of the cycle had been filed off the frame in an obvious attempt to make it difficult to identify, a second number – 103648 – was found on the inside of the front forks.

With the help of the BSA factory in Redditch, the police now managed to trace the bicycle to a shop in Derby, which had sold it to a customer called Ronald Light in 1910. The man had been lodging in Derby at the time, but had since

Ronald Light, who was tried for the murder of Bella Wright and acquitted.

returned to live at his mother's home, 52 Highfield Street, Leicester. When the police called at this address, they found that Light was now living in Cheltenham, where he was teaching at Dean Close School. Light turned out to be an ex-public schoolboy and an engineering graduate.

When interviewed, Ronald Light said at first that he'd never owned a green bicycle; then that he had owned one but he had sold it, and finally that he couldn't be expected to remember what colour cycles he'd owned at various times. During this ever-changing account, the only piece of his testimony that remained constant was that he had definitely not been in Gaulby on 5 July 1919 and that he had never met Bella Wright.

When both George Measures and James Evans picked out Light as the man they had seen waiting for Bella on the evening of her death, the police were sure they had the right man and he was charged with murder.

The trial in June 1920 was a major one. Ronald Light had been a soldier during the 1914–18 war. He had begun the war as a lieutenant in the Royal Engineers, and was referred to as Lieutenant Light throughout his trial, although he had lost his commission in 1916 and finished the war as a private in the artillery. As the government wanted to reassure the public that servicemen returning to civilian life were not a danger to life and limb, there was a policy of using very high-ranking barristers to prosecute in the case of ex-servicemen charged with serious offences. In the trial of Ronald Light, Sir Gordon Hewitt, the Attorney General, led the prosecution.

Representing Light was Sir Edward Marshall Hall, the foremost defence lawyer of the time. It looked as though he would have a hard task to defend Light, as the evidence against him was overwhelming. He was the proven owner of the green bicycle recovered from the canal. A cycle shop owner gave evidence that Ronald Light had brought in this cycle for repairs shortly before the day of the murder.

George Measures and James Evans identified Light as the stranger who was waiting in Gaulby for Bella Wright 20 minutes before she was found shot. The police had the accused man's conflicting accounts of whether he had ever owned a green bicycle.

The attorney general led the case for the prosecution and then inexplicably returned to London before Sir Edward Marshall Hall began his defence. The local barrister left in charge of the prosecution team was left floundering when the defence suddenly changed tack. Far from denying that Ronald Light was the man on the green bicycle – the case that had been put forward until that moment – Marshall Hall now admitted that his client was indeed the man in question. Ronald Light had been cycling in the area on the day of the murder. He had met Bella Wright, helped her to repair her cycle and then ridden along with her to her uncle's house in Gaulby. Yes, Light had spoken to Bella as she left her uncle's house at nine o'clock – though he denied addressing her by name – and he had ridden part of the way home with her, but then he had parted from Bella to take a different route and had left her still alive.

He admitted that the cycle parts recovered from the canal were his, and explained that he had disposed of them in a panic after reading the lurid accounts in the press about the man on the green bicycle pursuing and shooting the girl. Sir Edward Marshall Hall managed to sow sufficient doubt in the jury's mind for Ronald Light to be acquitted. He did not return to his teaching post in Cheltenham, as the testimonials used to obtain the post were found to be have been forged. He changed his name to Leonard Estelle, and lived on the Isle of Sheppey in Kent until his death in 1975.

The question remains: who did kill Bella Wright? The majority of people in Leicestershire still believe that Light was the killer and that he was lucky to have had a remarkable barrister who got him acquitted. After the trial, evidence began to emerge that he had a history of making approaches to young women. Two schoolgirls stated that he had tried to talk to them on the Saturday afternoon before cycling off and finding Bella Wright struggling with her bike chain. No one had ever explained how Light came to lose his commission in the Royal Engineers in 1916. Officially it was recorded as due to his 'lack of initiative', although no one had ever complained about his ability as an engineer. It has been alleged that he was reduced to the ranks after an incident in which he assaulted a young woman in France, but actual evidence is sketchy.

Other possibilities have to be examined though. In 1982, A. W. P. Mackintosh, a writer from Evington, self-published a slim booklet called *The Green Bicycle Mystery*. In it he puts forward the possibility that Bella was not murdered at all, but accidentally shot by someone culling crows in the fields alongside the Via Devana. He quotes an incident from his childhood, when he and a friend – both boys were about 14 – were shooting in a field. The two boys had got hold of a couple of .45 revolvers and some ammunition, and were firing indiscriminately in a field, when someone walked down the lane. This incident occurred in 1919, the same year as the shooting of Bella Wright, and Mr Mackintosh points out how many service revolvers from the 1914–18 war were around at the time. If someone was shooting in the field when Bella Wright was cycling down the lane, it is possible that a bullet could have gone through the hedge and hit her. However, the only evidence for this hypothesis was the large black bird found at the spot where Bella was killed. Mackintosh postulates that it might have been shot by the same mystery shooter in the field, but this theory is weakened by the fact the PC Alfred Hall, who first saw the bird, stated that it had gorged itself to death on the blood at the scene. And PC Hall was nobody's fool, as proved by his enterprising and courageous actions on the day after the killing. However, Mackintosh's booklet did have some benefits. He managed to track down the whereabouts of the green bicycle frame, to the wall of a shop in Evington. Moreover, he used the profits from the sale of the booklet to erect a stone in Stoughton churchyard, on the previously unmarked grave of Bella Wright.

One third possible explanation for Bella's death presented itself to me in December 1995. I was signing copies of a previous book which mentioned the case, in W. H. Smith in Leicester's Gallowtree Gate, when a lady approached me and said, 'I see that you think that Ronald Light did the murder.' She then went on to introduce herself as the daughter of one of Archie Ward's sisters. She told me that the murder case had led to her having a very restricted childhood; she was never allowed to go out unaccompanied. She then made the startling comment, 'Most of the women in our family, though not the men, think that Uncle Archie might have done it!' She explained that Bella's young man might have come home on leave unannounced and been overcome with jealousy when he saw his girl cycling with another man. In this scenario, he waited until the man cycled off on his green bicycle, before shooting Bella himself.

I have considerable doubts about this theory. Although I have no reason for doubting that the lady was who she said she was, she didn't seem old enough to be Archie Ward's niece, unless her mother was much younger than Archie. Also, I believe – or at least I hope – that the police would have checked out the whereabouts of Bella's fiancé at the time of the crime.

Of the three possibilities I have outlined, the most likely one is that Ronald Light, the man acquitted by the court, was indeed the killer. If so, it is ironic and against all natural justice that he lived a full life up to the age of 89, while his victim died before her 22nd birthday.

RED COMYN

Lord Comyn of Whitwick Castle was a notorious man, a member of a Scottish clan who had fought on the English side against Robert the Bruce. He was a giant of a man with great strength and prodigious appetites. His long red hair and beard led to his nickname – Red Comyn. He spent his days fighting and his nights drinking and womanizing. No local pretty maiden was safe from his clutches. If she took Red Comyn's fancy, she didn't stay a maiden very long. Fathers with young daughters dreaded the day that Red Comyn would suddenly notice how attractive they were.

One young woman who caught the eye of Red Comyn was Agnes Ferrars, the pretty young daughter of Lord Ferrars of Groby Hall. When in 1304 he made his intentions clear, Agnes was horrified and refused his advances. Never a man for the subtle approach, Lord Comyn had his men seize her and carry her off, but as they approached Whitwick Castle she took her chance and escaped. When Comyn heard, he flew into a rage and sent his men to recapture her, promising a reward to the man who brought her to him and a hanging to all of them if they failed. An anonymous local poet, writing in the early 19th century, described how Agnes fled through Charnwood Forest with Comyn's men in hot pursuit:

The oaks of the forest were Autumn tinged,
And the winds were at sport with their leaves
When a maiden traversed the rugged rocks
That frown over Woodhouse Eaves.

The rain fell fast – she heeded it not –
Though no hut or home appears;
She scarcely knew if the falling drops
Were raindrops or her tears.

Onward she hied through the Outwoods dark,
And the Outwoods were darker then;
She feared not the Forest's deep'ning gloom –
She feared unholy men.

Lord Comyn's scouts were in close pursuit
For Lord Comyn the maid had seen,
And had marked her mother's only child
For his paramour, I ween.

When Agnes heard the men shouting and whistling up
on Buck Hill, near Nanpantan, she realized they were very
near, and she hid in a hollow oak tree. A storm began, and
whenever a flash of lightning lit up the area around the
tree, Agnes could see her brutal pursuers searching for her.
She said a prayer to the Virgin Mary, asking that she
should remain safe from the lustful intentions of Red
Comyn.

A whistle, a whoop from the Buyk Hills' side
Told Agnes her foes were nigh,
And, screened by the cleft of an aged oak,
She heard quick steps pass by.

Dark and dread fell that Autumn night;
The wind gusts fitful blew;
The thunder rattled; the lightning's glare
Showed Beacon's crags to view.

The thunder neared – the lightning played
Around that sheltering oak;

Groby Hall, the family home of Agnes Ferrars.

But Agnes, of God not men afraid
Shrank not at the lightning's stroke!

The thunder passed, the silvery moon
Burst forth from her cave of cloud
And showed in the glen Red Comyn's men
And she breathed a prayer aloud.

'Maiden mother of God look down,
List to a maiden's prayer.
Keep undefiled my mother's sole child –
The spotless are thy care.'

The next day, when the hermit who lived by Holy Well
Haw looked out, he saw what appeared to be a girl's corpse
lying on the ground. He carried her to his well and, using a
scallop shell, he sprinkled water from the holy well over her

Holy Well Haw, pictured in 1841.

deathly white face. To his joy, he saw her eyelids flutter and her lips move. He realized that the 'corpse' was in fact still alive. He managed to get word back to Lord Ferrars, and the girl was borne back to Groby Hall.

> The sun had not glinted on Beacon Hill
> Ere the Hermit of Holy Well
> Went forth to pray, as his wont each day,
> At the cross in Fayre-oke dell.

> Ten steps had he gone from the green grassy mound
> Still hemming the Holy Well Haw,
> When stretched on the grass, by the path he must pass,
> A statue-like form he saw.

> He crossed himself once, he crossed himself twice,
> And he knelt by the corpse in prayer:

'Jesu Maria! cold as ice –
Cold, cold, but still how fair!'

The hermit upraised the stiffened form,
And he bore to the Holy Well:
The Paters or more he muttered o'er
And he filled his scallop shell.

He sprinkled the lymph on the maiden's face
And he knelt and prayed at her side.
Not a minute's space had he gazed on her face
Ere signs of life he spied.

The next spring, the same hermit was walking near the
well early one morning when he saw a young couple riding
on horseback towards him. After each drinking a shellful of
water from his well, they blessed the hermit, and the lady
introduced herself.

Spring had invested the Charnwood oaks
With their robe of glist'ning green,
When on palfreys borne, one smiling morn,
At the Holy Well Haw were seen

A youth and a lady, passing fair,
Who asked for the scallop shell;
A sparkling draught each freely quaffed
And they blessed the Holy Well.

They blessed the Well, and they fervently blessed
The holy hermit too;
To that and to him they filled to the brim
The scallop, and drank anew.

'Thanks Father, thanks, to this well and thee,'
Said the youth, 'but to heav'n most

I owe the life of the fairest wife
That Charnwood's bounds can boast.

The blushing bride thou seest at my side,
Three hours ago made mine,
Is she who from death was restored to breath
By heav'n's own hand and thine.

The prior of Ulverscroft made us one,
And we hastened here to tell
How much we owe to kind heav'n and thee
For the gift of the Holy Well.

In proof of which, to the Holy Well Haw
I give, as a votive gift,
From year to year three fallow deer,
And the right of the challenge drift.

I give besides of land, two hides,
To be marked from the Breedon Brand,
To be held while men draw from the well in this Haw
A draught with the hollow hand.'

The hermit knelt, and the hermit rose,
And breathed Benedicte –
'And tell me,' he said, with a hand on each head,
'What heav'n sent pair I see?'

'This is the lost de Ferrars' child,
Who dwelt at the Steward's Hay;
And, Father, my name, yet unknown to fame,
Is simply Edward Grey.'

Not only does the poem give a frightening insight into
the character and activities of Red Comyn, it also explains
how the Grey family – the ancestors of Lady Jane Grey,

England's nine-day queen – first came to live at Groby Hall.

Another version of the story names the girl as Alice, rather than Agnes. Like the first story, this one places its heroine at Groby Hall, but Alice is a wealthy and attractive young widow. Red Comyn's lust is combined with avarice, since Alice owns valuable lands that border his. Comyn's men try to seize her from Groby Hall when she's there alone, but she manages to escape. Heading through Charnwood Forest, she tries to make a circuitous route for Grace Dieu Abbey, but gets lost. She hides from her pursuers in a hollow oak tree, before fainting close to the hermitage at Holy Well Haw. The next morning she is found by a hermit, who bathes her face with the cold pure water from the well, and she is revived.

Holy Well Haw (*haw* means enclosure) had a hermitage since the early 1100s. It is now a farmhouse, but the water from the spring still flows cold and pure. The farmhouse, owing to a mapmaker's error, was later known by the grander title of Holywell Hall, but is now simply Holywell Farm. Visiting it in April 2002, I was given a drink of water from the well, now bricked in and piped to the farm, by Sue and Richard Smith, who live there. It was as cold and pure as it was when the hermits lived there in the days of Agnes Ferrars and Red Comyn.

Despite his failure to capture Agnes (or Alice), the wild behaviour and amorous conquests of the terrible giant Lord Comyn continued throughout his life. He died in a fight at the age of 34, but after his death a new and terrifying story began to spread. Among the crags of High Sharpley and in the forest of Charnwood, a huge wolf was lurking. This wolf had a taste for the flesh of young maidens, and the creature was covered in long red fur! The local people soon put two and two together and the belief was established that Red Comyn – now in vulpine form – was still chasing girls. Versions of the story differ; so whether the wolf simply ate the girls, or whether he transformed into his human shape and ravished them first, is somewhat blurred. Over the years, a new element was added: the wolf was virtually immortal and the only way the life of the wolf could be ended was if it was killed by a virtuous young maiden of royal blood.

The wolf carried on eating girls down the centuries and it was not until the 1550s that the matter was resolved. Lady Jane Grey, the great-granddaughter of Henry VII, was walking in the grounds of Bradgate Hall with friends. Lurking nearby was a huge wolf, said to be the last wolf in Leicestershire. Needless to say, it had long red fur, and the sight of the 14 year old Jane seemed to excite its attention. It stalked her, and then attacked. One of Jane's young companions, Francis Beaumont of Grace Dieu Hall, tried to defend her. It is possible that Francis was in love with Jane, though his feelings were of no account to her parents, who were plotting with the Earl of Northumberland to marry her to the earl's son and seize the throne when the sickly young King Edward VI died.

Francis drew his hunting knife and threw himself at the wolf. He managed to stab the giant beast in the side, but the wolf threw him off and returned to its preferred prey, Jane. With no thought for her own safety, the girl seized a rock and hit the wolf over the head. Temporarily stunned, the animal fell to the ground, but then its jaws opened in a savage snarl. Jane picked up a branch from an oak tree and thrust it into the open mouth. With a piercing howl, the wolf leaped to its feet and then fell down dead. Lady Jane had slain the wolf and, if the legends are true, she had also finally rid Leicestershire of Red Comyn, the beast of Whitwick.

It seems strangely fitting that the maiden who finally killed the wolf was a direct descendant of Edward Grey and Agnes Ferrars, the girl who had narrowly escaped the lustful intentions of Red Comyn, in the forest by Holy Well Haw.

Red Comyn was not the only Lord of Whitwick Castle to spend his life chasing and ravishing young maidens. Some while after the time of Lord Comyn, the lord of the castle was Goisfried Aslin. He brought many of his female conquests to live at the castle, where they enjoyed, temporarily, a life of leisure and pleasure. They were referred to as Lord Aslin's jillflirts. One young woman who took his fancy was a local Whitwick girl called Gertrude Lyne. His usual practice was to seduce the girl with soft words or to take her by physical force, but on this occasion, when Gertrude resisted, Lord Aslin decided to pay court to her. Eventually he even asked her to marry him. She was aware of Goisfried Aslin's reputation, but was secretly flattered and, ignoring her family's warnings, she agreed to wed the notorious lord. After all, Goisfried had promised her that he would become a reformed character after the wedding, a well-worn line used by suitors throughout the centuries.

For a few months after the marriage, Lord Aslin did appear to be a changed man, but the improvement in his conduct did not last. He was soon back to his old tricks, but now things were even worse. He forced his horrified young bride to watch the orgies that took place at the castle. When she protested, he informed her that in a month's time, he would expect her to participate fully in the licentious activities that he and his friends enjoyed.

As the month passed, he continually reminded Gertrude that the day was coming when she would have to join in, adding that he and his lustful friends were all looking forward to it. The night before the dreaded day, Gertrude sneaked out of the castle and ran away. Her body was found in a nearby lake next morning. Whether she had fallen in accidentally or had taken her own life in desperation was never known. There is one other possibility. Goisfried Aslin was not only a lecher, he was also a brutal egomaniac. He did not tolerate anyone who disobeyed his instructions. It is possible that he was aware that his young wife was about to run off and had her followed and killed. After all, he was becoming bored with the virtuous young girl.

Whether she died in an accident, as a suicide, or as a murder victim remains a mystery. Whitwick Castle is long gone, remembered only in the name of Castle Hill. However, Gertrude's ghost is said to still haunt the area to the east of Whitwick, particularly near Blackbrook and Gun Hill House, a remote gamekeeper's cottage, uninhabited since 1950, when Eric and Nellie Cook left. The cottage is built into the rock and can be seen from Oaks Road, an eerie silhouette against the skyline, a lonely and fitting haunt for the ghost of the young Lady Aslin.

Gun Hill House, said to be haunted still by the ghost of Gertrude Lyne (Whitwick Historical Group)

A MURDEROUS WALTER MITTY

For me, one of the mysteries about any domestic murder is how anyone can be driven to kill a member of their own family. I know, of course, that the majority of murders are domestic, and perhaps I am just lucky in my close relatives. One of the most heinous of domestic crimes must be matricide: the murder of one's mother. And when matricide is combined in a double murder with patricide, the evil seems compounded to an incredible degree.

When Derek and Eileen Severs disappeared from their Rutland bungalow in November 1993, it wasn't their 37 year old son Roger who reported the fact to the police, but their worried neighbours. Derek and Eileen were a retired couple in their late fifties, living in that part of the county that is a peninsula, almost an island, on Rutland Water. Its uniqueness and beauty made the location highly sought after and the bungalow a very worthwhile investment.

Derek Severs was a former ICI executive, who took his retirement gently. Every lunchtime would find him in the Finch's Arms in the village of Upper Hambleton. Eileen, a retired dental nurse, was much more active, getting involved with many community activities. She was a member of the Rutland Volunteer Bureau, Age Concern, and the Citizens Advice Bureau. When she wasn't playing golf at North Luffenham, she was teaching the inmates of Ashwell prison to play bridge. Indeed, she had been awarded the MBE in 1989 for her charitable work in the community. Both Derek and Eileen, in their different ways, were enjoying their life in retirement.

Despite his public school education, Roger hadn't made much of his life. He'd had a series of short-term jobs as a barman, a crop sprayer, and an assistant in an ironmonger's shop, but often boasted to strangers that he was a successful businessman or a doctor. The contrast between his real life and his imaginary high-flying life pointed to a Walter Mitty attitude.

After a series of failed relationships, he had met Jain Galliford in 1990 through the personal columns of a local newspaper, telling her that he was a gynaecologist, though he later changed this story to one in which he was an

Derek and Eileen Severs at Buckingham Palace for the award of Eileen's MBE. (Leicester Mercury)

agricultural salesman. The two became lovers, and had a son. Roger moved in with Jain and, for a time they ran a hotel together in Lutterworth, but by April 1993 Jain, fed up with his constant lies and his need to control everything, threw Roger Severs out. He returned to Upper Hambleton to stay with his parents.

Roger kept asking his father for money to set up a new business, but Derek Severs refused, deciding that he had bailed Roger out too often already. Derek also added that Roger should move out of the bungalow and find a place of his own. Although his father paid the rent of a flat in Oakham for him, Roger was not happy. When he discovered that his father had lent £10,000 to a former landlord of the Finch's Arms to enable him to buy another pub in Langham, he was filled with rage and resentment. Derek had lent money to an acquaintance, but would not help his own son. In Roger's mind, it wasn't fair.

When Derek and Eileen disappeared, Roger continued to live in the bungalow. He told some neighbours that his parents had gone on holiday, but told other people that his father had suffered a stroke and had gone away to recuperate. He sent Jain Galliford a bunch of red roses, and then took her out for a romantic meal, paying for the meal with a roll of banknotes. He told her that his parents were away but that he had sorted out his long-standing disagreements with them. He spoke about marrying Jain and buying a pub of their own.

In the village, people who knew of Roger's permanent disregard for the truth, grew concerned about the couple's absence, and the police were informed. When officers came to question him, they found Roger Severs sitting by an open fire, looking very much at ease and at home. Although Roger insisted that his parents had gone to London for a break, they were not satisfied. Both the Rover and the VW Golf were still in the garage, and it seemed unlikely that 20 stone Derek Severs, who suffered from arthritis, would have gone anywhere without his car. Another factor which made the police suspicious was that the kitchen and bathroom carpets had disappeared. Roger's explanation was that his father had spilt fat in the kitchen and his mother had let the bathroom tap overflow. When forensic scientists found traces of blood in the bathroom, Roger had no explanation. Despite the fact that there was no sign of the bodies, Roger Severs was arrested and charged with the murder of his parents.

The search for the bodies began with the excavation of the bungalow's garden and paddock, and then widened to include Rutland Water itself. Rutland Water is a man-made lake with a perimeter of 24 miles; so this was a considerable task. Special sonar equipment had to be borrowed from a neighbouring water authority, but the search proved fruitless. The breakthrough came when Dr Tony Brown, a lecturer in geography and archaeology at Leicester University, was called in to examine soil found under the wheel arches of Derek Severs' Rover. He discovered that it contained pollen and plant particles that could only have come from a wooded area on the Hambleton peninsula. The search now concentrated on the local woodlands, and two bodies were discovered in a shallow grave in Armley Wood. The male body had been wrapped in a blanket, and bound with string and two belts. The female body had a jumper pulled over the head. Both victims had had their pockets emptied and turned out. The soil covering the bodies proved to have come from the paddock at the bungalow. The police concluded that Roger Severs had used his father's car to transport his parents' bodies to the wood, and then made several journeys to take soil from the bungalow to the wood.

Dr Clive Bouch, the consultant pathologist, found that both victims had been battered to death with a hammer or mallet. Neither of them had been able to defend themselves, and the first blows may have been struck from behind. He also noted that Mrs Severs may have lived for some time after the attack. When Roger Severs was visited on remand in prison, he showed no reaction to the news that his parents' bodies had been found.

The murder trial took place in November and December 1994, a year after the crime. The prosecution case was that Derek had battered his mother with a hammer in the bathroom of the bungalow, then left her dying while he

Roger Severs, a murderous Walter Mitty. (Raymonds Press Agency)

went outside to wait for his father to drive home from the pub. He had attacked him as he climbed out of the car, hitting him ten times. He had then put his father's body on the back seat of the Rover, and his mother in the boot. During the night he had made numerous journeys to Armley Wood, taking first the bodies and then several loads of soil to cover them. The next day he had made a systematic attempt to cover up the murders, burning clothing, disposing of bloodstained carpets, and thoroughly cleaning the car and garage. He even delivered a number of raffle prizes that his mother had been about to take.

Roger Severs admitted killing his parents, but told the court that he was guilty of manslaughter owing to diminished responsibility. He said in the days before the killing, he had been drinking excessively. On the actual day, he had gone to the bungalow to speak to his mother about a possible reconciliation with his former partner Jain. When his father returned from the Finch's Arms he made offensive remarks about Jain and himself. He had followed his mother to the bathroom, still carrying a steak mallet with which he had been tenderizing some meat for tea. After his mother had made further comments he struck her. When his father ran outside, he had followed him and struck him too. He had very little recollection of the events, but when the cold air eventually brought him to his senses, he found that both of his parents were dead.

A defence psychiatrist gave evidence that Roger Severs was clinically depressed at the time of the killing, but this was refuted by a psychiatrist acting for the prosecution. Dr Peter Wood said that Severs was a Walter Mitty type of character, but added that he was a callous, detached individual 'who lies and cheats and can be aggressive'. He described him as being 'unreliable, untrustworthy, boastful and grandiose, claiming attributes he does not have'.

The jury found Severs guilty of murder, and he was sentenced to life imprisonment.

After the trial, Jain Galliford, the mother of Roger Severs' young son, said that, had he got away with the murders of his mother and father, she herself would have been his third

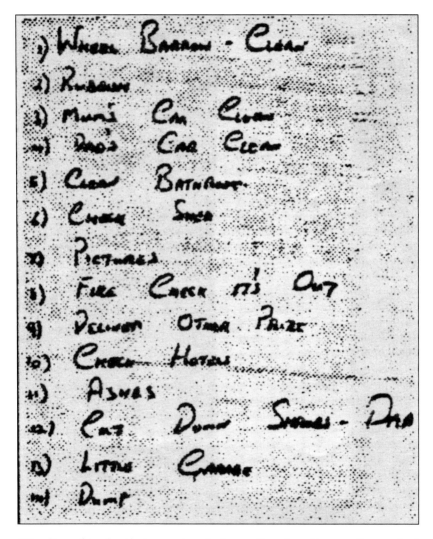

The list of tasks that convinced the police that Rogers Severs had murdered his parents.

victim. In a moving tribute to Eileen Severs, Jain said, 'She was the best thing that ever happened in my life. She was a lovely and a wonderful lady and I miss her terribly.'

As well as the question of how a man can bring himself to murder his parents, there is for me another mystery. Roger Severs may been domineering and deceitful, but he was not unintelligent. After the murder, he made a numbered list of 14 things he needed to do to hide the crime. He carried out these tasks thoroughly, even recruiting the unwitting help of his parents' gardener and a 13 year old boy. But then this intelligent man failed to destroy the list. He left it in the bungalow, where it was found by the police and produced as evidence in court.

This incredible blunder might make one wonder whether Roger Severs wanted at a subconscious level to be found out. Or perhaps the truth is more prosaic. He may have thought that he had plenty of time to dispose of the list, not realizing that the concerned neighbours would fetch in the police as soon as they noticed the disappearance of Derek and Eileen. It might be that Roger's reputation as a pathological liar set alarm bells ringing in the village at a much earlier point than he had calculated.

TWO RARITIES OF NATURE

People have always been curious about those fellow humans who are in some way out of the ordinary. Long before the American freakshows were invented, anyone of unusual size was regarded with fascination. They were given the title of 'rarities of nature', or occasionally 'miracles of nature', a less unpleasant epithet than 'freaks'. Rutland and Leicestershire had, between them, one of the smallest and one of the largest human beings who ever lived.

The latter was the Leicester jail keeper, Daniel Lambert, who weighed over 50 stones. Daniel was born in Leicester's famous Blue Boar Inn in March 1770. He had two sisters, who, like his parents, were of normal size, though he did have an uncle and aunt on his father's side of the family who were very large. The uncle was described as the largest man in Leicester, but Daniel was to take over that title later. As a boy Daniel was tall and well built, but not unusually heavy. He liked sport and was a keen swimmer.

Following an apprenticeship with a button engraver in Birmingham, Daniel returned to Leicester at the age of 18 to assist his father, who was the keeper of the County Bridewell, the 'house of correction', in Blue Boar Lane. Three years later, he took over his father's position as the jail keeper. He was about 5 feet 11 inches tall, still of normal weight and enjoyed a full social life. He bred dogs and fighting cocks, took part in hunting and other field sports, and was in appearance a sturdy but athletic man. However, during the next two years something abnormal happened, and by 1793 his weight had shot up to 32 stones and was still increasing. This was not due his intake of food and drink, since he was not greedy, eating only one course at any meal, and he never drank alcohol. He remained at this time a strong man, and was reported to be able to easily lift a weight of a quarter of a ton.

In 1805, when Daniel was 35 years of age, he had reached 53 stones in weight. When the prison where he worked closed, although his employers declared 'the universal satisfaction Daniel Lambert had given in the discharge of the duties of his office', he was not offered a post at the new prison. This was almost certainly due to his size. The Leicester magistrates granted him a life pension of £50 per annum, but this was not enough to keep him in comfort. His only option was to make money by offering himself for public exhibition.

After a carriage had been specially made to transport him, he moved to London, there taking apartments at 53 Piccadilly. He received visitors between the hours of 12 noon and 5 pm, charging them a shilling to come and see 'the heaviest man who ever lived'. This rather high fee was obviously to keep out the riff-raff. With a body circumference of over 9 feet, and each leg having a circumference of over 3 feet, Daniel Lambert proved a great attraction with Londoners. He was reported to receive his paying guests with great courtesy, conversing with them with wit and conviviality. One visitor later wrote: 'When sitting, he appears to be a stupendous mass of flesh, for his thighs are so covered by his belly that nothing but his knees are to be seen, while the flesh of his legs, which resemble pillows, projects in such a manner as to nearly bury his feet.'

While he was in London, he met another Leicestershire man, the artist Ben Marshall. Marshall painted Daniel Lambert's portrait, and the two men became good friends, Ben Marshall even naming one of his sons Lambert. However, being a curiosity on show may not have been entirely to Daniel's taste, since, after only five months in

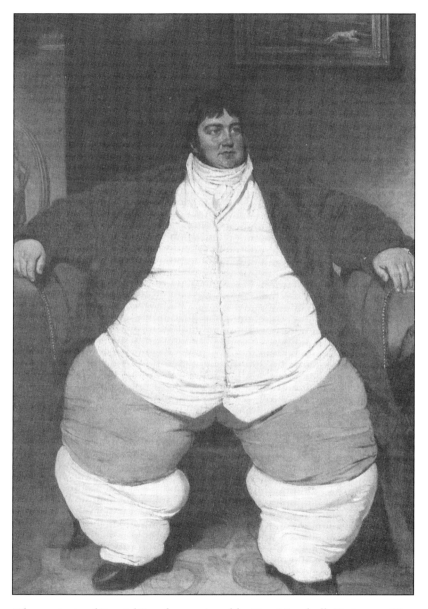

The portrait of Daniel Lambert painted by Ben Marshall. (Leicester City Museums)

London, he decided to return to a quieter life in Leicester, where he lived for another four years. He did not allow his great size and weight to restrain him in one place and, using his special carriage, he travelled to Birmingham, Coventry, Cambridge and Huntingdon. Daniel had a passion for horseracing, and at the age of 39 he died on a visit to Stamford races, while staying in ground floor rooms in the Waggon and Horses Inn.

To remove his body, the wall and window of the inn had to be removed. It was decided to bury him in Stamford, as returning his body to Leicester would involve too many logistical difficulties. His enormous coffin was 4 feet wide and built from 112 feet of elm. Mounted on wheels, it was taken down a ramp to the grave in the churchyard, where it took 20 men 30 minutes to slowly lower him to his final resting-place. A gravestone erected by his many Leicester friends marks his grave in St Martin's churchyard.

In the Newarke museum in Leicester visitors can see his enormous waistcoat and breeches, together with his armchair and walking stick. Also in the museum is the portrait by Ben Marshall and a collection of caricatures. Despite the fact that the big man was a teetotaller, Leicester has a Daniel Lambert pub in Gamel Road, while Stamford has one in St Leonard's Street.

In contrast to the Leicester giant, Jeffrey Hudson, born in Oakham in 1619, grew to an adult height of only 3 feet 9 inches. In fact he was only 18 inches high until the age of 30. Perhaps it is apt that Rutland, England's smallest county, should produce this smallest of men. Although sometimes referred to as the Rutland dwarf, or the queen's dwarf, Jeffrey was not at all misshapen. He was a perfectly formed, though miniature, man.

Jeffrey's father, John, was an Oakham butcher, and George Villiers, the Duke of Buckingham, also employed him to provide bulls for bull-baiting, then a popular sport. When Jeffrey was seven years old, he was presented

A portrait of Jeffrey Hudson.

to the duchess. She was enchanted by the tiny boy and took him into her home at Burley House, just outside Oakham. His country clothes were replaced by tailor-made apparel in satin and silk, and he was given two servants of his own.

Jeffrey rose to even higher status following a banquet given by the duke to entertain King Charles I and his 15 year old French queen, Henrietta Maria. It has been suggested that this actually took place at the duke's London residence, but the local tradition in Rutland has always been that it happened at Burley House. During the meal, what appeared to be a large venison pie was brought out and placed on the table before the royal guests. A trumpet sounded, and the young Jeffrey Hudson, clad in a miniature suit of armour, burst out through the piecrust. To the amazement of the guests, the tiny boy walked up and down the table waving his tiny sword. One version of the tale tells how Jeffrey then walked up to the Duke of Buckingham and with a show of daring impudently tweaked his nose. The startled duke went to hit the boy, but the king, almost crying with laughter, intervened and told the duke it served him right for imprisoning the child in the pie. Jeffrey later stated that he had not enjoyed being in the pie, especially when it was put into the oven to warm it up!

The young queen took an instant liking to the boy, and took him back to London with her. The queen's household contained a number of what were then called 'rarities of nature', including her porter, William Evans, who was 7 foot 6 inches in height. The sight of the 18 inch boy from Rutland standing next to the lofty porter must have been startling. Little Jeffrey became an absolute favourite with the ladies of the court, who spoilt him with their attentions. For a while Jeffrey became very conceited and self-important. Indeed, when his father came to court, Jeffrey refused to acknowledge his relationship to this humble Rutland butcher. The king, hearing of the boy's behaviour,

Sir Anthony Van Dyke's portrait of Queen Henrietta Maria with Jeffrey Hudson.

had the boy beaten, and over the years Jeffrey did learn to curb the worst of his arrogance.

Henrietta Maria kept her own household at Denmark House. She had a great love of plays and masques, and even acted in them herself, to the disapproval of the general public. They also disapproved of the fact that Denmark House was an island of Roman Catholicism in a Protestant London. Jeffrey Hudson took part in many of the masques and plays. In one play, the enormous William Evans, playing the part of the giant Gargantua, sits down to eat. He pulls a loaf of bread from one pocket, then from the other he produces Jeffrey Hudson! The audience must have found it hilarious.

Jeffrey had his portrait painted by many of the royal court painters, including Daniel Mytens and Sir Anthony Van Dyke. One of Van Dyke's portraits shows the queen with little Jeffery and a pet monkey. The monkey is sitting on Jeffrey's arm, attached to him by a blue ribbon, and Jeffrey is connected to the queen by an identical blue ribbon. In his fascinating book, *Lord Minimus*, Nick Page points out the significance of this. The monkey belongs to Jeffrey and is his pet. In the same manner, little Jeffery belongs to Queen Henrietta Maria; he is her pet.

Jeffrey took part in all the court activities. He learned to ride and hunt, to fence and shoot, to dance and act. He became the perfect miniature courtier, charming and witty. In 1630, the 10 year old Jeffery accompanied a royal mission to France to bring back a French midwife for the queen. On the way back pirates captured the party and took them to Dunkirk, which was then an independent Flemish state. However, the captives were too important to hold for long, and they were soon released into France, whence they were able to return to England. It was while in Dunkirk that Jeffrey is supposed to have fought a battle with a turkey-cock, although this may have been made up later by the poet William D'Avenant, who mocked the whole adventure in verse. If it did really happen, it was not a subject for ridicule, since the fierce bird must have been much larger than the 18 inch tall boy.

When the Civil War broke out, Jeffrey was keen to do all he could to support the king and queen. When the queen went to Holland to raise money for the Royalist cause, Jeffrey was by her side. When, under fire from enemy ships, she took shelter in the port of Bridlington, there too was Jeffrey. She even made him a Captain of Horse, a title he used with pride throughout his life. It is possible that Jeffrey fought at the Battle of Newbury in 1643. When the queen had to flee England to live in exile in France, Jeffrey was of course one of her companions.

However, while there he fell into disgrace when a man named Charles Croft began mocking his size. When Jeffrey challenged him to a duel, Croft thought he was joking, but he was deadly serious. The duel went ahead, the men, mounted on horses, using pistols. Jeffrey was an expert shot and his tormentor was killed. The queen's dwarf was not a man to ridicule; he had no sense of humour, especially when he thought he was being mocked. Jeffrey's punishment for the death of Charles Croft might seem a light one, but for him it could not have been worse. He was banished from the queen's court-in-exile. He had to leave his beloved Henrietta Maria, and, although he did not know it at the time, he would never see her again.

Jeffrey tried to get back to England, presumably to see if he could rejoin the Royalist army. But once again, as he tried to cross the Channel, pirates seized his ship. This time the pirates were the real thing: Barbary corsairs. The prisoners, including little Jeffrey, were taken to North Africa and sold into slavery. Jeffrey was 25 when this happened, and he spent a further 25 years as a slave. During this terrible period of his life, an amazing thing happened: he began to grow. Less than 2 feet tall when he became a slave, he grew to 3 feet 9 inches by the time he was 50! He later attributed this increase in height to the beatings he received and the change in his diet.

In 1669, Jeffrey Hudson returned to Rutland, where he probably lived with his brother Sam. In his absence from England, he had missed the execution of Charles I, the Commonwealth of Oliver Cromwell, and the restoration of the monarchy under Charles II. Henrietta Maria had come back to England as the queen mother, but a combination of ill health and unpopularity for her religion had made her go back to France.

In 1676, after the death of his brother, Jeffrey went to London to see if Charles II would treat him as well as his father had. However, it was the time of anti-papal hysteria arising from the lies fabricated by the Machiavellian Titus Oates – who, ironically, was also a man from Oakham in Rutland. Jeffrey Hudson was accused of participating in the Popish Plot and was imprisoned for two years. However, it is recorded that he was paid money, £50 in 1680 and £20 in 1681, from a secret service fund. It seems likely that he ended his days as a spy working for the government, but what he actually did to earn this money is shrouded in mystery.

Unlike the 53 stone Daniel Lambert, who lived for only 39 years, Captain Jeffrey Hudson, the little man from Oakham, lived to the age of 63.

MAD, BAD AND DANGEROUS

The phrase 'mad, bad and dangerous to know' was originally applied to Lord Byron, but that particular aristocrat had many redeeming features, amongst which was the fact that he often spoke up in Parliament for the poorer members of society.

However, Laurence Shirley, the fourth Earl Ferrers, had fewer virtues and many more vices. He inherited his title in 1745, at the age of 25, and with it he inherited estates in Leicestershire, Derbyshire and Northamptonshire. His residence, however, was at Staunton Harold Hall in north-west Leicestershire.

One of his vices was his prodigious appetite for alcohol, and this addiction may well have been the basis for other unpleasant habits. He had an overwhelming and terrifying temper, which caused him to act violently towards other people, particularly his servants. In common with most aristocrats of the period, he saw nothing wrong in this; the lower classes existed solely to serve their betters. When one of his servants refused to back him in an allegation that a tradesman had sold him some bad oysters, Earl Ferrers beat the man with a candlestick, and then stabbed him with a knife. On another occasion, when guests failed to turn up to dine with him, he threw objects at everyone in sight before kicking and horsewhipping his servants.

It was not only the servants who feared him; his fellow peers also despised and disliked him, regarding him as insane. Earl Ferrers' excommunication from the Church must have been an embarrassment to his family, especially to his younger brother, the Reverend Walter Shirley. Few people wanted anything to do with this eccentric and unpredictable earl, and none would welcome an invitation to visit Staunton Harold Hall.

As well as his consumption of alcohol, Ferrers had other appetites too; he lusted after the company of women. One that particularly caught his eye was Margaret Clifford, the daughter of his land agent. Whether the girl's father objected to her seduction is not recorded; in any case, it would not have mattered to Earl Ferrers. He first took the girl to his bed in 1743, and she bore him four children between 1744 and 1749. It didn't matter that these were all daughters; they were illegitimate and had nothing to do with inheritance.

Staunton Harold Hall, the home of Laurence Shirley, Earl Ferrers.

For the continuation of his line, he would have to make a suitable marriage and produce male heirs. In 1752, he married Mary, the 16 year old sister of Sir William Meredith of Henbury, in Cheshire. Perhaps Cheshire was far enough away for the Meredith family to have been ignorant of Earl Ferrers' reputation, or it may be that he was of such high rank that it was not a factor. Earl Ferrers was later to claim that the Meredith family tricked him into the marriage by making sure that he was drunk at his engagement, drunk at his wedding, and drunk for the whole the period in between. Since there was hardly a day in his life when he was not drunk, this ungallant claim was a bit rich.

Needless to say, the marriage was not a happy one. Earl Ferrers abused his young wife, both physically and verbally. He also terrified her by sleeping with a loaded pistol under his pillow, telling her that he might decide to shoot her during the night.

His treatment of his wife was so brutal that Parliament granted her a legal separation. This was an unusual event in the mid-18th century and is an indication of the extent of Earl Ferrers' reputation for madness and brutality. Part of the act of separation was that Lady Ferrers should receive an income from the rents of certain farms. For this to be put into practice, it was necessary for the trustees to appoint a trustworthy man to oversee the arrangements. Not surprisingly, there were no volunteers. Whoever was appointed would have to be independent enough to make sure that the wild earl was obeying the instructions; not an easy task.

Eventually the job went to John Johnson, an upright and sober man, who was Earl Ferrers' steward. When Johnson was reluctant to accept the position, it was Earl Ferrers who persuaded him, saying that he wanted it to be done by someone he could trust. Initially things went well, but it wasn't long before the mercurial peer changed his attitude, accusing poor loyal Johnson of plotting with the trustees to cheat him. The trustees had to intervene to prevent Johnson being evicted from his cottage. The accusations became wilder, until Ferrers became convinced that John Johnson was having a passionate love affair with Lady Ferrers, an idea that everyone else knew was ridiculous.

Things seemed easier when Earl Ferrers called at Johnson's cottage with a small gift and a request that the man should come up to Staunton Harold Hall on the following Friday at 3 pm. Johnson did as asked, but when he arrived at the hall he found that all the menservants and Margaret Clifford and her children had been sent away and there were only three maidservants present. Earl Ferrers made Johnson wait outside for ten minutes, then called him in and locked the door. Some time later, the three servants heard Earl Ferrers shouting angrily, followed by the sound of a gunshot. Earl Ferrers emerged and calmly told one of the women, Elizabeth Doleman, to see what she could do for Johnson, who had been shot in the side. She took the injured man to lie down on a bed, but Earl Ferrers – no longer calm – burst into the room, seized Johnson by the hair, and threatened to put a bullet through his head.

When he was calm again, Ferrers sent for Margaret Clifford and told her that he had shot John Johnson, justifying the action by saying that the man deserved it because he wouldn't admit his guilt. Earl Ferrers also sent for Sarah, Johnson's daughter, and told her that if Johnson died he would make financial provision for her, provided that no legal proceedings were taken. Earl Ferrers' moods swung backwards and forwards between rational behaviour and insane rage, but eventually he was persuaded to send to Ashby-de-la-Zouch for the local physician, Dr Kirkland.

When the doctor arrived, he could see that John Johnson was dying, but he had enough sense of self-preservation not to say so. Earl Ferrers refused to allow the injured man to be removed from the hall, but when he fell into a drunken sleep Dr Kirkland left, returning with a number of men and a chaise. He had Johnson taken to his own cottage, where he died the next morning. The doctor now had a moral predicament. The man had been murdered, and it was his duty to take action. However, the murderer was Earl Ferrers, the local aristocrat, who regarded himself as above the law. It might have been the easy option to keep quiet, but the doctor was a man of principle. He went back to Staunton Harold with several burly colliers and disarmed Earl Ferrers, who was waving a gun about and threatening to shoot anyone who came near him.

Ferrers was taken to the White Hart Inn in Ashby and an inquest brought in a verdict of wilful murder. He was taken to Leicester jail, but a local court could not try him. He must be tried by his peers – literally – and he was taken to the Tower of London to await trial by the House of Lords.

In the two months before his trial, he lived in the Round Tower, with two wardens in the room with him at all times

Maggie's Cottage, Lount, once the home of John Johnson. (John Bowler)

and another outside the door. Other than that, he was treated well, with all the privileges of his rank. His mistress, Margaret Clifford, took lodgings nearby, and wrote to him daily. Although she was not allowed to visit him, their four daughters were. While in the Tower, Earl Ferrers cut down his drinking, imbibing a mere drop of brandy with his breakfast, a pint of wine with his dinner, and another pint with his supper. Moderation indeed! This diet of two pints of wine a day and a little brandy does give some hint as to his previous intake. While in custody Earl Ferrers did one good deed. He made his will, leaving £6,000 to his illegitimate daughters, to be paid when they married or reached the age of 21. He also left £1,200 to Sarah Johnson, the daughter of the man he had shot dead.

The trial began on 16 April 1760, in the Westminster Hall of the House of Lords, before the Lord High Steward, Lord Henley. The Attorney General, Sir Charles Pratt, and the Solicitor General, Sir Charles Yorke, led the prosecution. Among those giving evidence were Dr Kirkland, Sarah Johnson and the maidservants who were present at Staunton Harold Hall at the time of the murder.

Earl Ferrers was required to conduct his own defence. His family had dissuaded him from claiming that the shooting of John Johnson was justified, which was his own view. Instead they persuaded him to claim that he suffered from bouts of insanity. He found plenty of people to support this claim. Almost everyone who knew him – family members, servants, tradesman or acquaintances – agreed that his behaviour was so bad they all thought he was 'cracked in the head'. One witness was a Peter Williams, who gave an account of what happened after Earl Ferrers came to collect a mare that he had left in the care of the Williams family. The earl was not satisfied with the condition of the animal, and proceeded to knock Mrs Williams to the ground and to run Peter Williams through with a sword, causing him a serious injury. At this point the Solicitor General intervened to say that this was no proof of insanity or eccentric behaviour. After all, he pointed out, if a man couldn't take such action against a negligent servant, then everyone present would be in the dock.

Earl Ferrers presented his case well. So well, in fact, that his fellow peers decided that such an articulate man was obvious completely sane. He was therefore guilty of murder and was sentenced to be hanged at Tyburn. This annoyed Earl Ferrers. It was not so much the death sentence that outraged him; it was the fact that he would be executed in the manner of a commoner. He petitioned the king, claiming that someone of his rank was entitled to be beheaded, but the petition was never answered.

The hanging took place on 5 May, after a procession through the streets of London. The hanging of a peer was an unusual event and everyone wanted to be able to say that they were there. Grenadier guards led the procession, followed by Earl Ferrers in his own landau, accompanied by Sheriff Vaillant and the chaplain of the tower. Other notables followed in their own carriages. The crowd was so dense that the short journey took almost three hours.

Earl Ferrers mounted the scaffold with the aplomb that suited such an important event, but an unfortunate incident spoiled the occasion. Since a hanging in 1760 did not involve a long neck-breaking drop, it was the custom for any wealthy man about to be hanged to give a sum of money to the hangman. In return, a man would be posted under the platform to pull on the legs of the hanging man and speed up the strangulation. On this occasion, however, Earl Ferrers gave five pounds to the wrong man, and a brawl took place between the hangman and his assistant. A man as proud as Earl Ferrers must surely have been aware of the lack of dignity involved.

There is a widely quoted belief that Earl Ferrers was hanged with a silken rope, but there is no foundation for the myth. He was, however, hanged wearing the white silk suit with silver embroidery which he had worn for his wedding, because he held that it was his marriage that had led him to the scaffold. After being dissected and put on display – the normal practice with executed men – his body was buried in St Pancras church; 22 years later, it was brought back to Staunton Harold, and was reinterred in the impressive surroundings of the family vault. In contrast, the body of John Johnson lies in an ordinary grave in the churchyard in Breedon on the Hill. Even in death, rank plays its part.

But was Earl Ferrers mad or just bad? Arthur Crane, in his excellent book, *The Kirkland Papers*, argues that Earl Ferrers was probably a schizophrenic, and that today he would not have been convicted of murder. I would hesitate to disagree with Arthur Crane, a retired solicitor as well as a local historian, but it seems to me that Ferrers had planned the shooting of his steward quite rationally. On the Sunday,

The tombstone of John Johnson in Breedon on the Hill churchyard.
(John Bowler)

five days before the murder, he had called on Johnson, feigning amiability and inviting him to the hall. On the Friday, before Johnson arrived, Ferrers had sent away his mistress and children and all menservants. This seems to me to show careful planning. After the shooting, he offered Johnson's daughter money if she would undertake not to prosecute him, which indicates he was still thinking logically.

I would agree with Arthur Crane that Ferrers' alcoholism played a major role in both his personality and in the committing of the crime, but I would add both arrogance and a belief that he was above the law to the ingredients. For me, he was more bad than mad, though I must concede that others may think the opposite. On one thing everyone would have to agree; mad *or* bad, Earl Ferrers was certainly 'dangerous to know'.

TOPSY TURVEY, WRESTLER AND MURDERER

The small hamlet of Bilstone lies in the west of the county, between the villages of Congerstone and Twycross, famous for its zoo. About a mile from Bilstone is an unusual reminder of Leicestershire's brutal past, namely a wooden post about 7 feet high, though, as the top is broken, it was obviously even taller at one time. A notice attached to the post informs the passer-by that it is a Leicestershire gibbet post and that the last person suspended from it was John Massey, in 1801.

Massey was a local hedger and ditcher, but he was much more famous under his nickname of Topsy Turvey. This unusual sobriquet came from his activities as a wrestler, and his claim that he could take any man from four counties, turn him upside down – topsy-turvey – and throw him over his head to the ground. The four counties were Leicestershire, Derbyshire, Staffordshire and Warwickshire, because Bilstone is quite close to the spot where the four counties meet. About 8 miles away, in the village of No Man's Heath, is a pub called the Four Counties, alleged at one time to have had a room in each of the four counties. The drinkers there used to move from room to room to take advantage of the different drinking hours in each county.

John Massey was a strong man, but he was also a bit of a thug, enjoying using his strength to intimidate others. He had few close friends, though he did have a number of drinking companions, as he was very fond of ale. His first wife had died, but no one knows how; neglect or bullying may well have played a part. He then married a widow with a 10 year old daughter. A few months after the marriage, Massey was on his way home after a daytime drinking session when he met his new wife and his stepdaughter on the road. What passed between them is not recorded, but it may have been along the lines 'You're drunk again, John!' or 'You're so late that I've given your dinner to the dog!'

Whatever the exchange, the wrestler became enraged and beat up his new wife so badly that her legs were broken. He then picked her up, carried her to Bilstone Water Mill and threw her into the millrace, where the poor woman drowned. Her little daughter tried to intervene, and she too was thrown into the water. Fortunately, she swam to the edge and survived to give evidence against her stepfather when he was tried for the murder of his wife.

He was tried in Leicester and after a very short trial was found guilty. As he was sentenced to death, he came out with a breathtakingly crass request: would the judge make sure, he asked, that after he was hanged his body be laid to rest between those of his two wives. He obviously thought that these two ladies, at least one of whom he had brutally killed, would miss his presence in the graveyard.

He did not get his wish. After the hanging at Red Hill, near Birstall, his body was taken back to Bilstone and put on the gibbet. It should be noted that there was a difference between the scaffold and the gibbet. The scaffold was where the felon was put to death, hanged until dead. The gibbet was where the dead body, bound in chains or metal bands, was put on display. As in the case of John Massey, this was often near the place where the crime had been committed, and was meant as a terrible warning of what would happen to those who broke the law. The 13th century practice of publicly displaying the bodies of executed criminals on a gibbet was re-introduced by the Earl of Leicester in 1753, and was finally abolished in 1834.

I once thought that these gruesome public displays were for a short period, a few weeks or at worst a few months, but John Massey's body remained on the gibbet post at Bilstone for an incredible 18 years. Obviously it decayed, and it was a skeleton that hung there for most of that period. Although it was meant as a deterrent, it has to be said that the wrestler's former drinking companions got into the habit of staggering back from the pub with an extra pint which they proceeded to pour down what was left of his mouth.

Today, souvenir hunters keep stealing the notice from the gibbet post, which gives the details of the case. In the first two decades of the 19th century, there existed the same sort of vandals, because eventually John Massey's skull was taken. Local stories insist that the man who stole it had it lined with silver and used it as a drinking vessel. One lady

The gibbet post at Bilstone, where the body of John Massey hung for 18 years.

from Congerstone told me that the skull ended up in a public house in Atherstone, where it was brought out once a year on Shrove Tuesday, on the occasion of the town's annual ball game.

The area around the gibbet post is said to be haunted by the ghosts of both the brutal wrestler and his victim. In March 2002, after I had spoken to the members of the local Women's Institute, a lady informed me that her brother had seen the ghost of a man carrying something heavy towards the water mill. Could it have been the ghost of John Massey still carrying his wife to throw her into the millrace?

Another witness, an Irish lady from Birmingham, told me that she came to find the Bilstone gibbet post after reading about it in a book. She admitted that it took her a long while to track it down, as she thought it was in the town of Bilston in the Black Country. When she eventually realized that the Bilstone she wanted was a small village in rural Leicestershire, she drove over to see it. She got out of her car and went over to read the notice. 'There was another lady there at the same time, with a little girl,' she informed me. 'The lady was reading the notice solemnly, though the girl was laughing and playing about. It wasn't until I was driving home that I wondered why the lady and girl were soaking wet, as it had been a dry afternoon.' My Irish acquaintance is now convinced that she saw the ghosts of John Massey's victim and her daughter.

SOLDIER-KING,
SHAKESPEAREAN VILLAIN

Leicestershire plays a large part in the story of Richard III. He spent the last night of his life at the White Boar Inn in Leicester, although that tavern did have a sudden change of name the next day. He heard his last mass at the church of St James in the village of Sutton Cheney. And he was killed on Sunday, 22 August 1485, at Ambion Hill, during the Battle of Bosworth Field. Leicestershire is Richard's final resting-place too; his remains – originally buried at Grey Friars in Leicester – were later disinterred by his enemies and thrown into the river Soar.

Many of Richard's problems can be traced back to the day in 1464 when his elder brother King Edward IV met and married a young Leicestershire widow. Elizabeth Woodville had married Sir John Grey of Groby Hall when she was 20, and had borne him two children. During the Wars of the Roses, Sir John fought on the Lancastrian side and was killed in battle. When the Yorkists triumphed, Sir John's property in Groby was forfeit. It was a penniless but pretty widow of 27 who met the young King Edward while he was walking alone on a visit to the East Midlands. Elizabeth begged the young king to allow her enough money to bring up her children with some degree of comfort. Edward, a tall, handsome 20 year old, looked at the widow of a former enemy and fell madly in love with her. Edward was used to having his own way with comely wenches, but Elizabeth refused to become the king's mistress, holding out for an offer of a more permanent nature. Despite the fact that his cousin Warwick was touring the continent to find a suitable royal bride for him, Edward married Elizabeth Woodville on 1 May 1464.

The marriage was kept secret for several months before Edward openly admitted what he had done. The news was not received well by the royal court, filled as it was with the successful followers of the Yorkist cause. Everyone thought that Edward, in marrying for love, had behaved no better than a peasant. Warwick, just returned from France with news of a marriage he'd arranged between Edward and the sister of the King of France, was outraged to find he had been made to look a fool. The old nobility regarded the Greys and Woodvilles, now given high rank as relatives of the queen, as provincial upstarts. One of the men who may well have thought Edward had behaved foolishly was his brother Richard, later to become Richard III in suspicious circumstances.

Edward IV and Elizabeth Woodville had a family of their own, and their eldest son, also named Edward, was proclaimed king when his father died suddenly in April 1483. The new king was only 12 years old, and under the terms of Edward IV's will his brother Richard was appointed Protector of the Realm. Although he was entrusted with the care of his two nephews, within a month Richard had young Edward V and his younger brother taken to the Tower of London, declaring that they were both illegitimate. His somewhat dubious argument was that his brother's secret May Day marriage to Elizabeth Woodville was invalid, since at the time Edward was already contracted to be married to another woman. Richard himself became king, and the two princes in the tower were never seen again.

However, supporters of the Lancastrian cause produced a new challenger to fight Richard III for the throne. This was the Welshman Henry Tudor, who was living in exile in

France. He traced his tenuous claim to the throne of England through his mother, a descendant of Edward III. Henry, with the financial and military support of the French king, landed in south-west Wales, and made his way through Wales, Shrewsbury, Lichfield and Tamworth towards Leicestershire. Richard's army made its way south into Leicestershire from his stronghold in Nottingham. The two armies met in battle on a Leicestershire field 2 miles south of Market Bosworth on Sunday, 22 August 1485.

On first examination, it might be assumed that Richard III had the numerical advantage, since he had around 8,000 men in his army. Henry had only 5,000 men, consisting of 4,000 French mercenaries, together with Welsh and a small number of English supporters.

However, these numbers do not include the 5,000 men of the Stanley family. Lord Thomas Stanley of Lancashire and his brother Sir William Stanley from North Wales were present at the Battle of Bosworth, but were uncommitted to either side. King Richard, watching the fighting down below on the plain of Redemore, could see that the battle was becoming bogged down into a grim struggle of attrition. He was aware that Lord Stanley was standing by on the fringe with a large body of men. When Richard saw Henry Tudor's standard and realized that the pretender to the throne was close to it, he made a momentous decision. He would force the issue and resolve the stalemate. He put on his helmet encircled with the gold diadem – sometimes referred to as his crown – and gathered around him his standard bearer and other close companions. Richard spurred his horse into action, leading a courageous charge down Ambion Hill towards the figure of Henry.

Some regard this action as foolhardy, others see it as gallant, but even his enemies have never called into question Richard's courage on the battlefield.

Richard's onslaught was so powerful that it took him right into the enemy ranks and he slew Henry's standard bearer with his lance. Richard continued trying to get to Henry to engage him in personal combat, but Henry's bodyguards barred the way and Richard was driven back. His horse became trapped in a marsh but he continued to fight on foot.

It was at this moment that Lord Stanley, now able to see which side was likely to win the battle, decided the time was right to take part. He sent his brother's soldiers down towards the fighting to support Henry Tudor. King Richard, the soldier-king, was surrounded but fought on bravely, until Sir William Stanley's foot soldiers hacked him down and killed him. After his death, the king's body was mutilated, then stripped naked and thrown over a horse to be taken back into Leicester in humiliation. It was at this stage that the White Boar Inn had a strategic change of name to the Blue Boar, since the white boar had been Richard's emblem, whereas the blue boar was the badge of the Earl of Oxford, one of Henry's supporters.

The traditional view of Richard III has been that he was a tyrant king, a devil incarnate, who murdered his two nephews to get his hands on the English throne. Unlike his tall, handsome elder brother, Richard was small, dark, and deformed, with a withered arm and a hunchback. He was jealous of his brother's wife, Elizabeth Woodville and, in order to prevent her ruling through her son, he imprisoned Edward V and his younger brother in the Tower of London, later sending his retainer Sir James Tyrell to have them murdered and secretly buried.

The two nephews in the tower had a sister, Elizabeth of York. When King Richard heard that his enemy, the upstart Henry Tudor, planned to marry the girl, he announced that he intended to marry her himself, despite the fact that he was her uncle and he had a wife still living. In fact his wife, Anne, died soon after the announcement, giving rise to speculation that Richard had poisoned her.

This image of Richard III owes much to the play by William Shakespeare. It is here that we get our picture of

Richard the deformed villain. However, it is puzzling that contemporaries of Richard had somehow never spotted his deformities. Although smaller and slighter than his brothers, Richard had fought bravely and well in battle, and was highly regarded as a soldier. It is true that one shoulder was stronger than the other, but this was probably caused by his skill as a swordsman. The withered arm and humped back – so symbolic of his supposed inner wickedness – only come to light 112 years after Richard's death. It has to be remembered that Shakespeare was writing in the reign of Elizabeth I, the granddaughter of Henry VII who defeated Richard. It is perhaps only natural therefore that he should present her grandfather as the shining white knight of the struggle, and his enemy, Richard III, as a demon twisted in body and soul. The character of the Shakespearean Richard is a wonderful creation, but he is essentially fictional. Shakespeare even has him killing the Duke of Somerset at the Battle of St Albans, when the real Richard would have been only two years old. Unfortunately, it is through the powerful creation of our greatest playwright that we derive the version of Richard that has lasted down the centuries.

Modern historians have more doubts. Many speculate that one of the reasons why Richard had his nephews taken to the royal apartments within the Tower was to prevent what always happened when a minor became king. Disputes and bloodshed would break out as various factions attempted to either control the boy-king or oust him; better to have him declared illegitimate from the start than to face years of indecisive rule. And Richard, like many at court, was deeply suspicious of Elizabeth Woodville and her family.

Richard, it has to be admitted, had a better claim to the throne of England than Henry. In fact, since all four of his grandparents were English, it can be claimed that he was the last entirely English monarch of this country. Richard reigned for only two years, and in that period he established himself as a good and popular ruler, introducing fairness in the law courts. He passed laws to prevent people who were accused but not found guilty of crime having their property

Shakespearean villain: Anthony Sher as Richard III (1984).

seized. He took steps to prevent corruption during the transfer of the ownership of land. Unusually for the period, he was known to have concern about the treatment of the poor, founding the Court of Requests for poor litigants, an act that may well have made him enemies among the wealthy nobility. He treated his friends with generosity and – perhaps unwisely – allowed his enemies to live to fight another day. When he visited provincial cities, he declined presents, saying that he wanted people's hearts not their money.

In his book *Conflict and Stability in Fifteenth Century England* (1969), Professor J. R. Lander writes, 'Richard was an able soldier and administrator, a cultivated man, fond of music and architecture, a patron of learning and deeply pious. He introduced into Parliament a useful programme of reforming legislation. Had he come to the throne through the normal workings of the succession he might well have enjoyed a long and successful reign. According to the Bishop of St Davids, writing in 1483, everywhere he went he was popular amongst the people.'

It is this Richard, wise and compassionate, who is commemorated by those attending the annual service of commemoration held on the nearest Sunday to 22nd August in the church of St James in Sutton Cheney. It is the good King Richard who is remembered and respected by the 2500+ members of the Richard III Society, founded in 1924 as the Fellowship of the White Boar.

Nevertheless, a question remains. What did happen to the young Edward V and his brother Richard after they were imprisoned in the Tower of London in 1483? Their bodies were never found, though it is certain Henry Tudor would have greatly wished to produce them to support the story that Richard III had caused their murder. It is possible that Edward died of natural causes; he was known to be suffering from a jaw infection at the time he was imprisoned. But what of the younger prince? It has been

The statue representing Richard III, the soldier-king, on display in Castle Park, Leicester.

suggested that he was either smuggled abroad, or allowed to live out his days in a monastery. When the imposter Perkin Warbeck appeared in the French court in 1492, he claimed to be that prince. The fact that King Henry worried at first that the claim might be genuine is an indication that he hadn't at that stage formulated his story about the murder of the two princes by Richard III.

Other suggestions as to the fate of the princes have included an accident on the river Thames during a bungled attempt to smuggle them out of the Tower. This at least might account for the fact that the bodies were never found. Others have speculated that they were indeed murdered, but not by Richard. Some blame supporters of Henry, since the boys' removal would have been as much in his interest as that of Richard, but there is as little evidence for Henry's guilt as Richard's. In his *Secret History*, the Reverend John Dening quotes the possibility that the murderer was an unnamed churchman who rose to high office under the Tudors. However, the evidence for this is gained from conversations between a medium and the dead Richard; so what weight we can attach to this depends on our belief in spiritualism and seances.

One of the most convincing cases for Richard's innocence occurs in Josephine Tey's novel *The Daughter of Time*. However, the mystery remains unsolved. Perhaps we should conclude that the verdict in the case against Richard III should be the Scottish one of not proven rather than a clear cut innocent or guilty.

One further footnote to the story of Richard III is widely believed in Leicester, and this relates to King Richard's bed. When Richard arrived in Leicester to stay at the White Boar Inn in August 1485, he brought with him his own royal bed. When he set off for Bosworth, the bed remained, as the king expected to return after a triumphant victory. After his unexpected defeat and death, the bed remained in the upper front chamber of the renamed Blue Boar. In the reign of

Queen Elizabeth, the landlord was Thomas Clark. Thomas's wife Agnes, an overweight lady, leaned heavily on the bed and a gold coin fell from under the bed. Thomas and Agnes investigated and discovered that the bed had a false bottom. Hidden in it they found a leather bag containing £300 in gold coins dating from the time of Richard III. The couple told no one that they had found King Richard's treasure, but people began to speculate when they seemed to have suddenly come into money. The now wealthy Thomas became Mayor of Leicester, and after his death in 1599, his widow continued to run the Blue Boar in High Cross Street. In 1605, a visitor named Harrison was staying at the inn. He paid compliments to the maidservant called Alice Grimbold, and in return Alice told him that Widow Clark had a secret store of gold. Harrison left, but returned a few months later with an accomplice, a seasoned thief named Bradshaw. The two men booked into the Blue Boar, and during the night they attacked and tied up Mrs Clark. In her private parlour they found a chest, which they unlocked with a key provided by Alice Grimbold. Inside was a fortune in gold and silver coins. The two men stole the money, giving Alice a reward for her help. Before they left, Bradshaw, not wanting Agnes Clark to be able to describe him to the authorities, returned to the bound figure of the landlady and cruelly strangled her. The next day, a customer discovered the body of Agnes Clark, and Alice was found tied up in the buttery. In Leicester, tongues began to wag among the criminal fraternity, and it was not long before Alice Grimbold, Harrison and Bradshaw were arrested. Harrison seems to have escaped punishment but Bradshaw and Alice were sentenced to death. Oral tradition has it that Bradshaw was hanged, but poor Alice, who had fallen for the silver tongue of a rogue, was burned alive.

The Blue Boar wasn't demolished until 1836, but the bed was taken away in the 18th century, first to a house in Redcross Street, then to Rothley Temple. In 1831, it was removed to Beaumanor Hall, near Woodhouse Eaves, but is now on display at the Manor House museum in Donington-le-Heath, near Coalville.

The field where Richard met his death has, like many battlefields, an atmosphere of its own. One lady who fell under its peculiar spell is Joanna Dessau, a retired headmistress. In the early 1980s, Joanna was on a coach bringing visitors to the village of Cadeby. They were on their way to a steam engine rally at the home of the vicar, the late Teddy Boston. When the coach arrived at Cadeby, everyone disembarked. It was at this point that Mrs Dessau began to feel disorientated. For her, the bright August sun disappeared, the weather turning overcast and gloomy, with a chill wind blowing. She could see nothing of the rally, simply the great trees looming over her. She began to mutter that she had to get to 'the hill', then shouted aloud for her friends to bring her a horse, as it was 'only a short ride away'.

Joanna's companions were quite alarmed and tried to calm her down, as she struggled through a hedge, calling out that it was only a mile away. They thought she must be having a fit, or possibly might be suffering from sunstroke, and they restrained her. For them it was a hot August day, but in Joanna's mind she was surrounded by grey skies. Even worse was the fact that she could hear the terrible din of battle: the clash of swords, voices shouting, the sound of men screaming and groaning. The hideous din lasted for over two hours. Then suddenly, she was back in the sunshine at the steam rally, with her anxious friends looking after her.

Joanna tells me that until that afternoon she was unaware that the location of the rally was near Ambion Hill, and she had no idea that the date, 22 August, was the anniversary of the Battle of Bosworth. Teddy Boston was able to tell Joanna that the day of the battle was unseasonally dark, overcast and chilly, and that the battle had lasted for two and a half hours. Joanna discovered that she had pointed out the very route taken by Richard III towards the field of battle. She recalls that she felt distressed that the coach did not take that route. While in her strange state of mind, she had worried her companions by bursting into inexplicable floods of tears while pointing out the route taken by the horse carrying Richard's dead body after the battle.

Some years later Joanna returned to the scene of her timeslip experience, but did not recognize anything at all. 'Everything was completely unfamiliar!' she says.

PANTHERS AND PUMAS

In April 2002, a young man camping in Grace Dieu woods had an unwelcome visitor. A large cat walked into his campsite and stood watching him, about 3 yards away. He described the animal as being panther-like, about the size of a Great Dane, with a long thick tail. The eyes of the big cat reflected yellow in the glow of the campfire. It watched him for a moment, then walked away. Chris Mullins of the Leicestershire and Rutland Panther Watch commented that the creature was too large to be a member of the leopard family and was possibly a hybrid. The fact that its eyes reflected yellow confirmed that it was a cat, since the eyes of a dog would have been more amber. He added that the rocky outcrops around Grace Dieu would be perfect for a big cat to be hunting, as there were plenty of rabbits and vermin. The cat must have taken the opportunity to approach the campsite to scavenge for food. Although this big cat may have been potentially dangerous, it would not compromise itself while there were plenty of rabbits available.

This sighting was just the latest in a whole series in Leicestershire and Rutland, going back many years. Many have been identified as panther-like, others seem to resemble a puma, and yet others have been said to be lynxes. Although panther is the commonly used generic term, some experts use the initials ABCs, which stand for alien (ie non-native) big cats. Chris Mullins advises that there may be circumstances – walking up to one while it is eating or chasing one into thick cover – which might turn it into a lethal adversary. The rule is never to corner or antagonize a big cat, but the same would hold true of many animals, including red deer during their rutting season.

On 30 January 2002, two sightings, one near Coalville and another in Aylestone, occurred at roughly the same time, proving that there is more than one big cat living wild. At 8.50 pm, Edward Kviekauska was driving slowly past the Birch Tree roundabout in Bardon when he saw an animal cross the road and disappear into the bushes. It was much too big to be a fox or a dog, and had a long black wavy tail. Referring to the much-discussed phenomenon of big cat sightings locally, Edward said, 'I never really thought about it before. I was neither a believer nor a disbeliever. I always thought it was possible, but now my mind is made up.'

At roughly the same time on the same day, a woman in the Aylestone area of south Leicester came face to face with a big cat. She was in her garden in Montrose Road when the security light came on and she saw the cat, about the size of a bull mastiff, only 3 feet away from her. It had piercing yellow eyes and small ears, and looked well fed and muscular. It seemed unconcerned by the nearness of a human being, simply standing and watching her, before wandering off. The woman said that she was frightened, but at the same time she couldn't take her eyes off it. 'It was big, black and shiny, and its tail was long and straight with a curl at the end,' she said. 'I knew straight away that it wasn't a dog. I've never seen a panther in the flesh before, but I've seen one in pictures and it looked like that.'

David Spencer, the Panther Watch co-ordinator for Rutland and east Leicestershire, commented that people were putting food out for foxes and this was beginning to attract panthers into urban areas. He thought the one seen in Bardon was in more typical panther country, since it was seen in the vicinity of a railway, and panthers often travel along railway lines. David also said that the sightings of two panthers within ten minutes of each other, and over 20 miles apart, showed that were at least two of them living in Leicestershire, though he thought that five was a more likely number. Panthers tend to use a limited hunting range, before moving on to an adjacent area. The exact range is difficult to define, and would depend on factors such as the habitat and food distribution, but it is certain that they would not be moving from one side of the county to another.

David Spencer said that Leicestershire and Rutland had more reported sightings than elsewhere because the police here took them seriously. PC David Toone, a policeman based in Oakham, confirmed this, saying 'We're pretty convinced there is a big cat in the wild in Rutland. We got the first report in 1994, and we've had 18 since then. They seem to centre on a disused railway line that runs through Rutland, which of course would be an absolute haven for small wildlife.' PC Toone added that there was no indication that the animal posed any danger to human beings.

Although David Toone has not seen a big cat himself, there are a number of police officers who have. In May 1999, an ABC was spotted by officers on patrol on the Leicestershire-Rutland border. They were at Leesthorpe, on the road from Melton Mowbray to Oakham, when a big cat with a long tail walked across the road in front of them. They described it as bigger than a fox or a dog, with cat-like features and a feline way of moving. They were interviewed by a police wildlife officer, himself a firm believer in the Leicestershire big cat phenomenon, who said that they were certain that they had seen a panther.

On 9 July 1999 at 3.45 am, a senior motorway patrol police sergeant came off the A46 onto the M1 near Leicester services, and spotted on the verge an animal about the size of a Labrador dog but with a tail longer than its body. He stopped the car about 25 yards away and watched the creature playing in the grass, like a kitten with a mouse. Realizing it was a panther, he radioed his control room to see if the CCTV cameras could pick it up. Unfortunately they could not get the bank of the slip road into view. After a few minutes, the panther realized that it was being watched and raced up the bank into the field. This animal was of the same size and appearance as one seen a few weeks earlier in Braunstone Park, about 2 miles away down the old railway line. This one was playing like a kitten too, indicating that it could be about a year old or just over. The police said that the M1 incident was the fourth sighting by officers in the past four months.

Of course there are sceptics. John Edwards of Oadby says that he believes people are letting their imagination run away with them. 'They see a black dog late at night, or even an ordinary domestic cat, and then convince themselves they've seen a panther. People are very gullible, in my opinion. I'll believe in them when someone shoots one and produces the body.'

Against this, it is necessary to balance both the quality and the quantity of the sightings. There were over 170 sightings reported in Leicestershire and Rutland in the year 2000 alone. In terms of quality sightings, quite apart from the police officers, ABCs have been positively identified by a retired squadron leader in Oakham, who saw a panther near the town's railway station, and a local doctor in Grimston, who was out shooting rabbits when he saw a black leopard-like cat near one of the numerous old railway tunnels in the area. One of the most convincing sightings took place near the East Midlands airport, near Castle Donington, and the man involved was Robin Roberts, the manager of Drayton Manor Zoo. He certainly knows his cats, and positively identified the one he saw as a puma.

One morning in December 2001, a woman was walking her one year old golden retriever along the Hermitage Trail, the old railway line between Oakthorpe and Donisthorpe. It was very quiet, with the sun just coming up, when she saw an animal about 100 yards away, coming towards her. At first she assumed it was another dog, although it had a rather rounded head like a puma, and was not walking like a dog. She bent to attend to her retriever and when she stood up again the animal had disappeared. She carried on walking towards Donisthorpe until she came to the church; she then turned round and began to walk back towards Oakthorpe. When she came back to the spot where she had first seen the animal, she glanced into a field on the left and saw it again. This time it was much closer and she could see that it was a big cat, much bigger than her dog, with a much smoother coat and a long upwardly curving tail. With its back towards her, the cat jumped up into a tree and began to groom itself. The woman felt apprehensive, as there was nobody else around, but she stood rooted to the spot, watching. After ten minutes the animal came down from the tree and walked away 'with a crouching movement'. Chris Mullins went over to the location soon after the sighting and examined the tree the big cat had climbed. He found scratch marks indicating that something large had climbed the tree. The top one was about 6 feet from the ground.

Other positive evidence for the existence of ABCs includes a pawprint measuring 4 inches by $3^1/_2$ inches, found in August 1998, at the Castle Cement quarry near Ketton, Rutland, an area of many previous big cat sightings. The print was very clear and had sunk nearly 16 inches into the ground. It bore no sign of claws, as might have been expected had it been made by a dog.

It does seem that panthers and pumas are able to co-exist in the wild, and judging from the sightings of possible hybrids, they may even be interbreeding. It is likely that their existence goes back to the 1970s, when new legislation made the keeping of captive wild cats more difficult. Many big cat breeders have admitted releasing panthers and pumas into the wild to fend for themselves, rather than apply for a licence. Oddly, the practice of releasing panthers and pumas into the wild was not made illegal until the mid-1980s. But could these creatures survive and breed in the wild? In the hills of north Staffordshire, a number of wild wallabies have survived and bred since the 1930s when they escaped from a private zoo, developing very shaggy coats to protect them from the cold weather. It's just as feasible for big cats to have done the same thing in Leicestershire and Rutland, eating rabbits and rodents, and occasionally attacking sheep.

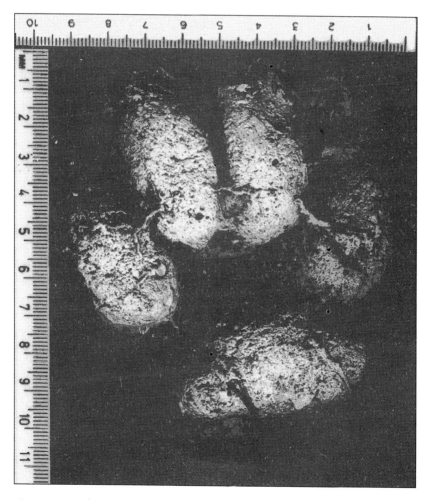

A pawprint found at Ketton Quarry in 1998. (David Spencer)

One of the most telling finds occurred when Mark Sentance, a wildlife enthusiast, made a discovery by a railway line near Great Dalby. The carcass of a sheep lay under a tree, with bloodstains and wool found high up in the tree. Although sheep can be killed by dogs and other animals, only a big cat would take one 12 feet up a tree to devour it. Mark made a video of his findings. He has also seen a panther not far from his home in Asfordby. Just before Christmas 2000, he was out with his two sons at 10 pm, trying to spot foxes on a bridlepath near the railway test track. They heard a commotion among a number of cattle in a field. The cows had formed a circle round their calves, while the bull was outside the circle, facing an animal the other side of the fence. Mark shone his powerful spotlight on the mystery animal, and saw a pair of bright yellow eyes. After several minutes the animal departed, and Mark saw its outline and recognized the clear silhouette of a panther. He returned to the spot at daybreak but was disappointed to find no pawprints to photograph.

I would like to return to John Edwards' comments about believing in panthers only when one has been shot. Leicestershire and Rutland are not the only areas of the country where ABCs are found. However, the cases here are very well reported and taken seriously by the police. This has led to one unfortunate side-effect. Trophy hunters are concentrating their search in Leicestershire and Rutland in their determination to obtain a unique 'ornament' – the head of a wild panther shot in England. Because of this, Leicestershire and Rutland Panther Watch, who are completely opposed to the killing of the counties' wild cats, have decided to be very cautious in the lists of sightings on their website (www.bigcats.org.uk/sightings). On advice from the police, they no longer put up sightings immediately they are reported, as this could lead hunters to the location.

So do the big cats exist? Everyone must make up their own mind. But sceptics are continually having to revise their opinions, like the Rutland businessman and his wife who saw a panther-like animal loping towards a railway line near South Luffenham at seven o'clock one evening in July 2001. They say, 'Well we used to be sceptics, but after what we saw that evening, we are now convinced converts. These big cats are definitely out there.'

NED LUDD

As the Liberty lads o'er the sea
Bought their freedom, and cheaply, with blood,
So we, boys, we
Will die fighting, or live free,
And down with all kings but King Ludd.

Lord Byron

In 1779, a man named Ned Ludd, or Ned Ludlum, lived in the Leicestershire village of Anstey. Ned was a bit simple; it was said in 1847 that he was 'of weak intellect'. One of the stories about Ned describes how one day he was being teased and taunted by a gang of village boys. Ned chased his tormentors into a frame knitting shop, but they disappeared. Thwarted, he vented his rage on one of the knitting frames and smashed it. Another version of the story says that Ned was actually the son of an Anstey framework knitter, and after being beaten by his father for laziness, he broke the frame he was working on. Whichever version of the story is true, what is certain is that whenever a knitting frame was broken Leicestershire people would say, 'Ned Ludd's been at it again'. Over the years, the phrase was used for any breakage. If you broke a cup, a cartwheel or a cooking pot, it was common practice to jokingly blame Ned Ludd.

Some 30 years later, his name was used again, this time by desperate men when they needed a fictitious leader, a Robin Hood figure, to keep their own names anonymous.

In the early 19th century, knitting was Leicestershire's main industry. In 1812, there were over 12,000 knitting frames being used, each frame providing work for the knitter himself, plus a bobbin winder and a seamer. As the knitting frame was usually situated in the knitter's own home, it is likely that the other two workers would be members of his family. The trade was controlled by men known as bag hosiers, who both provided the work and collected the finished garments. These same men owned the knitting frames and rented them out to the cottage knitters. During the Napoleonic wars, the framework knitting industry thrived for two reasons. One was that the need for soldiers drew many men from the knitting trade, leaving plenty of work for those who were left. The other was that the army needed a constant supply of knitted stockings for its soldiers. The bag hosiers installed more and more knitting frames, and agricultural workers began to take up framework knitting, which was better paid, as an alternative occupation. Knitting factories began to appear, in which a large number of frames were installed, instead of one in each cottage.

When, following a series of bad harvests, people bought fewer items of knitwear, wages fell and manufacturers looked for ways of cutting costs. A new process was devised of making large pieces of knitted cloth on very wide frames, and then making stockings by seaming and cutting them out. These garments, though inferior in quality, were much cheaper to produce. Moreover, they looked like the fully-fashioned garment, at least until they were washed and began to unravel.

The wide knitting frames were installed in factories, and men hired to work there. Those knitters still working in their own homes were forced to work for many more hours for far less money. Many of them lost their income entirely and had to apply for the low paid jobs in the knitting factories. In desperation, the knitters took to going into the factories at night and breaking the new machines. Letters were sent to the factory owners threatening to destroy their knitting machines, if they didn't pay the knitters a living wage and stop making the poor quality cut-up items. Obviously, the machine breakers didn't want to sign these threatening letters, not with their own names, at least. Instead they remembered the old sayings about Ned Ludd, the simpleton from Anstey, and many of the letters were signed 'General Ludd' or 'King Ludd'. From then on, the machine breakers were termed Luddites, and regular activists were called 'old Neds'.

It was not only in the knitting trade that the Luddites undertook their nocturnal activities. Lacemaking was another industry that had moved from cottage to factory and from being made by hand to being made by machine. In Loughborough, Heathcote and Boden's installed 55 lace-bobbin frames at their three-storey factory in Mill Street. Here, too, the out-of-work lacemakers were provoked into action.

Knitting machines at Wigston Framework Knitters' Museum.

The centres of Luddite activity in the Midlands were Nottingham, Leicestershire and Derbyshire, although in the north workers began Luddite activity against the weaving machines.

The authorities were terrified, seeing this as the beginning of a revolution. After all, the French Revolution had taken place in the 1790s, and it looked as though it could be repeated in England in the first two decades of the 1800s. The Combination Acts of 1799 and 1800 had made trade unions illegal, and it now seemed that the workers were taking direct action to improve their working conditions and raise wages. Although much Luddite activity was very localized, it was believed that travelling Luddites would come to an area to agitate and help to organize action. These men, it was alleged, signalled their presence in a new area by raising their right fist to their right eye; local activists, recognizing them, would reply by raising a left fist to the left eye.

Parliament rang with denunciations of the revolutionaries and Luddites, and only one voice spoke up in their defence. That voice belonged to Lord Byron, who said, 'Whilst these outrages must be admitted to exist to an alarming extent, it cannot be denied that they have arisen from circumstances of the most unparalleled distress. The perseverance of these miserable men in these proceedings tends to prove that nothing but absolute want could have driven a large and once honest and industrious body of the people into the commission of excesses so hazardous to themselves, their families and their community.'

In many communities, the Luddites had considerable popular support, a fact which alarmed the authorities even more. In an atmosphere of official panic, the army was brought into areas where Luddites were known to be active, and in 1817 capital punishment was reintroduced for the specific crime of smashing knitting frames. It is common today to think that most people who were hanged received that punishment for murder. It is interesting therefore to ponder the fact that of the 32 people who were hanged in Leicestershire between 1800 and 1837, only nine were murderers. The other 23 were found guilty of one of the other 200 offences that carried the death sentence: forgery, burglary, theft of a horse, hayrick burning and breaking a stocking-frame being but some of them. Rick burning and frame breaking were considered crimes against the state, revolutionary activities.

In 1816, John Heathcote introduced a powered version of a lace-bobbin machine into his Loughborough factory, which would make many men redundant and lower the rate of pay for the others. He was obviously expecting trouble and hired armed nightwatchmen to guard his factory. At midnight on 28 June, a band of Luddites broke into the premises by the rear entrance. One of the guards was injured and the other two were overpowered. The Luddites then smashed 55 machines and destroyed a quantity of finished lace.

Within a few days, the leader of the men, James Towle, was arrested in Nottingham, together with two other men, Ben Badder and John Slater. Towle and Slater were tried at Leicester assizes in August. Slater was acquitted, but James Towle was found guilty and sentenced to death. He showed great courage and fortitude on the gallows, and died without betraying the identity of any of his fellow Luddites. However, the following January, a member of the gang was caught poaching and bought his freedom by naming his companions.

The second trial took place in Leicester in April 1817. Two men were sentenced to be transported to Australia, but six more – William Towle (James's brother), Tom Savage, Bill Withers, John Amos, John Crowther and Josh Mitchell – were sent to the gallows. They were hanged together in Infirmary Square, before a crowd of 15,000 spectators. Public hangings were intended to serve as a warning to others, but on this occasion the crowd was sympathetic to the men and sang a hymn with them. It would be good, though highly unlikely, to think that the crowd might have sung Byron's *Luddite Hymn*, quoted at the beginning of this chapter, with its stirring line: 'And down with all kings but King Ludd!'

Whether the Luddites were class warriors taking direct action to further their justifiable political aims, or violent criminals foolishly opposed to technological change, is a matter of interpretation. In his booklet *The Loughborough Job*, Malcolm Hornsby postulates the theory that James Towle and his friends may have been a gang of poachers who were paid to attack Heathcote's factory. But who might have hired them? It is possible that it could have been rival Leicestershire factory owners, keen to get rid of the very successful firm of Heathcote and Boden. It could even have been Thomas Lacey, a former partner of John Heathcote. What is certain is that following the raid, Heathcote moved his operation to Tiverton in Devon, and the Loughborough factory was taken over by another manufacturer.

This was the end of Luddism in Leicestershire, and its members began to look to the Chartists to achieve their political aims. However, the word is regularly used to condemn anyone who opposes change in working practice. Although its use is almost always pejorative, it is interesting to know that whenever people refer to Luddites, they are using the name of Ned Ludd from Anstey in Leicestershire.

BUTTERFLY HALL

On the A4304 road from Market Harborough to Lutterworth, about a mile west of Lubenham, is the site of Papillon Hall. It was erected by David Papillon in 1624, substantially altered by Sir Edwin Lutyens in 1903, and demolished in 1950.

The many strange happenings at Papillon Hall all date back to the second David Papillon, the great-grandson of the original builder. This David was a handsome man, with a personality described as terrifyingly hypnotic and even psychic. The local population of his day was in awe of him, and called him Lord Pamp or Old Pamp, names for the devil. Papillon Hall has been known as Pamps ever since that time.

Lord Pamp had the power of 'fixing' or 'setting' people. Once, a footpad – foolish man – attempted to rob Pamp as he rode home from Market Harborough with a bag of money for wages. He obviously didn't know whom he was dealing with. Pamp set the thief, then coolly left the moneybag by the thief's feet, and rode home. There he stabled his horse and then sent the groom back along the lane to fetch the bag. When the servant picked up the bag, the transfixed footpad was released and able to run away. On another occasion, Pamp came across some men who were making a poor job of ploughing one of his fields; so he fixed them. They were unable to move at all until he came back at dusk and released them.

In the local area, any misfortune was attributed to the influence of Lord Pamp, and people would attempt to evade his evil eye by making the sign of the cross in the dough as they were making bread or in the mash when making beer.

A portrait of David Papillon, aged 24, was painted in 1715. This painting has had a peculiar effect on people ever since, including many who knew nothing of the stories surrounding Lord Pamp. Although his family sold the hall in the mid-18th century, the painting remained at Papillon Hall for another hundred years. In 1800, a servant girl was woken in the night by a sound she took to be a cat. Then, to her horror, she saw by the light of the moonlight coming through the window, Lord Pamp standing by the foot of her bed. He was dressed exactly as in his portrait, in a red coat and gold waistcoat, convincing her that David Papillon had emerged from the picture.

In 1840, Papillon Hall was owned by the Bosworth family but was lived in by a relative, a Mr Marriot. He begged Thomas Papillon to remove the portrait of his ancestor because of its sinister influence. He said that no servants would work at the hall, because Pamp used to come out of the painting and molest them. Thomas Papillon agreed to help and the picture was removed, first to Acrise Place in Kent, and then to Crowhurst Park in Sussex. However, all this achieved was to double the area of the hauntings, Pamp being seen both in Papillon Hall and in Crowhurst Park.

At Papillon Hall, George Atherton reported that many instances of crashing noises occurred during the period in the 1930s when he was butler to Captain Frank Belville. Even after the hall was demolished in 1950, Mr and Mrs Hewes, the owners of Papillon Farm, claimed that their stables were haunted by Pamp.

Crowhurst Park, the new place of residence for David Papillon's portrait, was also haunted by the figure from the picture. In 1900, Crowhurst Park was owned by Pelham Rawstone Papillon, but it was let to a Colonel Tufnell. In 1908, Pelham Papillon was amazed to receive a letter from the colonel's wife, begging him to take the picture away because of its evil influence. Pamp's portrait was taken to Pelham's home in Hastings, and from that time seems to have lost its sinister power. Lord Pamp seemed content to live in peace with his great-great-great-grandson, and no longer leaves his place on the wall.

The original Papillon Hall stood on raised ground and was an octagonal building with just one entrance. The roof was in the shape of a cross, and beneath it the top storey consisted of four gabled attics. The north-east attic, always known as Pamp's attic, was bricked up leaving just a small entrance hatch.

Before his marriage in 1717, Pamp kept a mistress, a woman of Spanish descent. She never left the hall, but used to walk on the leads of the roof. She died in 1715, but there is no record of her burial. However, when Lutyens was making the alterations to Papillon Hall in 1903, the skeleton of a woman was found in the bricked-up attic.

Papillon Hall after the extensive additions by Sir Edwin Lutyens. (David Carter)

Before the Spanish woman died, she uttered a curse that misfortune would occur if her dancing shoes ever left the hall. The shoes, which still exist, are actually a pair of silver and green brocade slippers fitted into a pair of pattens. The belief in this curse was so strong that whenever the house changed hands – it left the possession of the Papillon family in 1764 – the deeds required the new owners to keep the shoes at Papillon Hall.

This requirement has occasionally been ignored. When Thomas Halford was residing at the hall, he allowed the shoes to be taken to an exhibition in Paris. Subsequently, loud crashing sounds and other deafening noises from the drawing room were heard every night, and Halford tried to get the shoes back. Unfortunately for him, they had to remain in Paris for the whole 12 months of the exhibition. Life at Papillon Hall became so intolerable that the family moved out of the house until the shoes were brought back.

The potent dancing shoes that once belonged to Lord Pamp's Spanish mistress. (Leicestershire County Council)

When another owner, George Bosworth, died in 1866, the shoes were bequeathed to his daughter in Leicester. At Papillon Hall, the disturbances recommenced and terrified the family of the new owner, Lord Hopetoun. These continued every night until the shoes were obtained from George Bosworth's daughter and returned to Pamps. Only then was peace restored. A later owner had a strong cupboard constructed in the wall above the main fireplace, with a padlocked grill for a door. The shoes were now kept in this, visible but safely locked away.

When Captain Frank Belville bought the house in 1903, he decided to have it altered and extended. Lutyens was engaged, and decided to add four wings to the building to make it resemble a butterfly. *Papillon* is, of course, French for butterfly. He also added an extra storey, and while this was being built, the woman's body was discovered. Captain Belville was not superstitious, and had the shoes removed for safe keeping during the alterations. Immediately all hell broke loose at Papillon Hall. Many of the builders carrying out the work suffered serious accidents. Several were injured and eventually one was killed. No local men would work at Pamps, and Lutyens had to import workmen from further away. Captain Belville himself sustained a back injury when his pony-trap mysteriously turned over. He decided enough was enough; he retrieved the shoes from his solicitors' office and restored them to their place in the house. Equilibrium was restored.

However, people have short memories. Five years later, he allowed the shoes to go to Leicester Museum. In the days that followed, three polo ponies were killed by lightning, the hall caught fire, two servants died, and Captain Belville fractured his skull while hunting. The shoes were immediately fetched back from the museum, locked behind the grill, and, according to Len Beeny, whose father was stud groom at the time, the key was thrown into the lake.

During World War II, the hall was occupied by American

servicemen from the 82nd Airborne division. Some of the men, knowing that every day might be their last, decided to test the superstition. The grill was smashed open, and on at least two occasions a shoe was taken away. Each time, the man who took the shoe was killed, and his friends brought the shoe back to Pamps. After the war, one shoe and patten were missing, but when the hall was demolished in 1950, the missing shoe – though not its patten – was found under a floorboard. The two shoes and the one surviving patten were sent to Mrs Barbara Papillon, a descendant of the original owners, at Crowhurst Park in Sussex.

DNA Fingerprinting

One of the most important murder trials in Leicestershire was that of the man accused of having killed two teenage girls in the 1980s. Lynda Mann had been murdered in November 1983 and Dawn Ashworth in July 1986. Both murders had taken place on footpaths in the Narborough area.

Lynda Mann lived with her mother, her sister and her stepfather in Narborough. On Monday, 21 November 1983, she was murdered as she walked back from Enderby, where she had been to visit her friend Karen. She left Karen's house just before 7.30 pm and began to walk along a pedestrian shortcut (or jitty, as it is called in Leicestershire) which led between agricultural land belonging to Carlton Hayes hospital and a building site where houses were under construction. Because the lane had been tarmacked, it was known locally as the Black Pad. Her body was found the next morning at 7.20 am, about 12 hours after she had gone missing. She had been raped and strangled with her own scarf, and her body had been left near a copse of trees inside the hospital grounds. She was 15 years old. The police questioned and then released her stepfather, Eddie, who had spent the previous evening playing darts with an off-duty policeman in a local pub. When he came home to find that Lynda was missing, he had helped to search the area, including the Black Pad, though he had concentrated on the building site side.

The police believed the rapist was a youth or young man, and it seemed likely that he was a local man, given his knowledge of the local footpaths and shortcuts. In the weeks that followed, the Black Pad was provided with streetlights, and parents began to meet their teenage children off the school bus. But the weeks turned into months and then a year, and the inquiry was scaled down.

Two and a half years later, 15 year old Dawn Ashworth left her parents' home in Enderby to walk over to Narborough to call on her friends Sue and Sharon. It was July, the school holidays, and she had been working at her holiday job in the village newsagent's. She had had a good day, as a boy she knew had given her a present of a cuddly toy. It was Thursday and she had just been paid.

She had a choice of routes. Her mother liked her to take the one that went over the M1, then ran parallel with the motorway, and came out on King Edward Avenue. Her other route was much nicer, and was via a lane known as Ten Pound Lane or Green Lane, and across the fields of long grass, bushes and trees. Of course, Dawn knew about the terrible thing that had happened to Lynda Mann in 1983. But that was ages ago, and it had happened in the dark. Today was a sunny summer afternoon and it was only 3.30 pm. Terrible things didn't happen in broad daylight, did they?

Dawn reached Narborough safely, and called at Sharon's house, where she was told that Sharon had gone to call for Sue. At Sue's, Dawn was told that her two friends had gone for a walk round the village. She decided that she would give up the idea of trying to catch up with them, and began to walk home, again choosing Ten Pound Lane as her route.

She never got home. At five o'clock, Dawn's father received a phone call from Sue, asking to speak to Dawn. At half past seven he was getting worried, as Dawn had promised to be home by seven. At twenty minutes to ten, Dawn's parents called the police and reported her missing. Mindful of the earlier murder of a 15 year old in the same area, the police began an immediate search, but it was two days before the body was found, covered in hay, nettles and branches, in the bushes by Ten Pound Lane. Dawn, like Lynda, had been raped and strangled.

The police were sure that the same man had committed the two murders. They were interested in finding out the identity of a youth on a motorcycle who had been observed watching the search for the body, and eight days later they arrested a local youth who worked at Carlton Hayes hospital as a kitchen porter. When they discovered that he had described the location of the body before it had been made public they were sure they had the right man. All they needed was a confession. After a number of interviews totalling 15 hours, the youth confessed to the murder, then retracted it, and then confessed again.

What annoyed the police was that he would not admit to the murder of Lynda Mann two years earlier. They were convinced that both murders were by the same killer, and

The Black Pad in Narborough, the scene of Colin Pitchfork's first murder.

one of the officers had the idea of calling in a researcher from Leicester University. As an offshoot of his research into the genetic coding of muscles, Alex Jeffreys had discovered DNA fingerprinting. Within the body's chromosomes, every individual had his own unique 'bar code', inheriting half of it from each parent. DNA could be obtained from skin cells, hair and any body fluid. Since both girls had been raped, they had samples of the killer's semen. Alex Jeffreys could check the two samples and tell them whether they came from the same man.

He could and he did. The first news was what they expected: both girls had been raped by the same man. His other news, however, was shattering: neither girl had been attacked by the youth in custody. The police had extracted a confession from a man who had not committed the crime.

Now they had to start their inquiries again from scratch. After six months, a decision was made to use the talents of Alex Jeffreys again. On 1 January 1987, it was announced that the police intended to take blood and saliva samples from every male in the area who was aged between 13 and 31 at the time of the first murder. This would include everyone who lived in Narborough, Enderby and Littlethorpe, everyone who worked locally, tradesmen who called there, and all the male patients at Carlton Hayes hospital. Officially, it was voluntary, but public pressure was so overwhelming that no one took the theoretical path of refusing to attend. Altogether, the police took samples of more than 4,000 men and youths.

When a man who lived in Littlethorpe, a small village a mile south of Narborough, received his invitation to attend the council offices where doctors would take a sample of his blood and saliva, he began to panic. First he said that the date was inconvenient, and had it postponed. Then he began to consider what story he could give to a work colleague to persuade him to give the samples in his place. The first man he approached refused, but a second one agreed. He was safe.

By August, it seemed that the decision to take the samples had been an expensive failure. But in the Clarendon public house in Leicester, an interesting conversation was taking

LEICESTERSHIRE CONSTABULARY

COMMUNICATIONS CENTRE
ST. JOHNS,
ENDERBY,
LEICESTER, LE9 5BX.

From the
2nd November 1986 our
telephone number will
be changed to
Leicester (0533) 530066

OUR REF.

YOUR REF.

Dear Sir,

You will be aware by now that a large scale Police enquiry is taking place in this area to trace the person responsible for the tragic deaths of two local girls, Lynda Mann aged 15 years and Dawn Ashworth, 15 years. The success of this operation can only be achieved by the whole hearted assistance and co-operation of the community and it is to this end we are making a direct approach to you.

For elimination purposes we are endeavouring to obtain certain samples from the male population of the area. These samples will consist of blood and saliva only.

The samples will be obtained by fully qualified Medical practitioners and when the examination of the samples has been completed, they will be destroyed. The taking of the samples will comply with the strictest medical standards.

THE GIVING OF SAMPLES IS COMPLETELY VOLUNTARY

Your co-operation in this matter is sought, therefore, you are invited to attend the Blaby Rural District Council Offices, Narborough/Danemill School, Mill Lane, Enderby between 7.00pm and 8.30 pm on

..... _Thursday_ .... the .._22nd January_..

It would be helpful if you could be in possession of some form of identification in addition to this letter when attending.

If you are under 17 years of age, you must be accompanied by your parent or guardian.

If you are unable to attend on the date indicated, please telephone Leicester 482405 (Inspector THOMAS) when an alternative date will be arranged.

Thank you for your assistance.

A. Painter

A. PAINTER - Detective Superintendent

The invitation to give specimens for genetic fingerprinting.

place. Four workers from Hampshire's bakery were having a drink and they began to talk about a colleague called Colin Pitchfork, who was a bit of a womanizer. One of the four, Ian Kelly, then told the others that Colin had persuaded him to take a blood test in his place. Another said that Pitchfork had offered him £200 to do the same thing, but he'd turned him down. Kelly said that he had not been offered money, but had been told a tale of how Colin had taken the test in place of someone who was afraid of needles, but now that he had received his own invitation, he was afraid that his good turn would get him into trouble.

Jackie Foggin was amazed and disturbed. The others were talking about the blood tests connected to the Narborough murder investigation. This was serious. On the other hand they were talking about Colin Pitchfork, a man they all knew and worked with. Obviously he couldn't be the double killer. Jackie thought she would ask advice from the son of the publican, who was a policeman, the next time she saw him. Somehow he was never around, and after worrying about it for six weeks, she eventually rang the police with her information.

On Saturday, 19 September, Ian Kelly was arrested, and after the police had spoken to him a number of police officers went to Littlethorpe to arrest Colin Pitchfork and charge him with the two murders. Pitchfork admitted his guilt, and gave a detailed description of how each murder had taken place. At the time of the first killing, he had dropped his wife off at her evening class and then parked his car with his baby son in the child seat while he looked for a girl. Hardened police officers were shocked at his unconcerned manner, especially when he told them that, after the second killing, he had returned home and baked a cake. One creepy feature of his manner was that when a new officer came into the interview, Pitchfork started his whole story again so that they didn't miss any of the unpleasant details. He actually thought the girls were largely to blame, since when he had flashed at them they had backed away in the wrong direction.

Colin Pitchfork was later diagnosed as a psychopath of a psycho-sexual type. He could imitate good behaviour and even seemed to possess a certain charm, but this masked deviant and unfeeling actions. He showed no signs of anxiety or distress and was completely unable to show empathy. He had no ability to understand the feelings of others, and, although he could repeat verbal statements of regret, these would have no meaning for him.

Colin Pitchfork was tried in Leicester in January 1988, found guilty, and given two life sentences for the murders and two ten year sentences for the rapes. He also received a three year sentence for the conspiracy with Ian Kelly. Kelly was perhaps fortunate to receive a suspended 18 month sentence for his actions. Even the judge may have felt he was being lenient, as he added, 'I just about believe you did it because you accepted the story put forward by Pitchfork.'

The judge praised Alec Jeffreys for his discovery of DNA genetic fingerprinting, and the system has been used in many cases since. It can provide almost complete proof of guilt and it is possible to feel that verdicts today are more sound because of it. The release of the youth who had confessed to the Narborough murders was the first in a line, since genetic fingerprinting is also valuable in proving innocence. Alec Jeffreys gained a professorship at Leicester University and was later awarded a knighthood for his pioneering work.

The case of Colin Pitchfork will always be remembered as the first use of DNA fingerprinting in a murder trial. And yet, the ironic fact is that Pitchfork was *not* caught by the scientific certainty of this new and valuable discovery. He was caught because of his fear of it and the action he took to avoid taking the blood test. If Ian Kelly had not gossiped about it in the pub, and if Jackie Foggin had not been public spirited enough to repeat that gossip to the police, the truth may never have come out.

This contrasts with the case of another Leicestershire man, Tony Jasinskyj, found guilty of the rape and murder of a Hampshire schoolgirl called Marion Crofts in 1981. The case had gone cold, and it was only solved in April 2001 when Jasinskyj was arrested by Leicestershire police for assaulting his wife. The police did a routine DNA test, and were amazed and delighted when the sample was a perfect match with material taken from the dead girl 20 years earlier. Samples of semen taken from her body in 1981 now proved to be from the man from Desford. He was tried in April 2002, and jailed for life. Sir Alex Jeffreys' discovery had triumphed again, but this time it was the bio-technology, rather than a man's nervousness about taking the test, which proved the conclusive factor.

THANKS AND ACKNOWLEDGEMENTS

I would like to thank the *Leicester Mercury* for allowing me to use their cuttings library, and the *Loughborough Echo* for letting me appeal for information about the legend of Holy Well Haw. I would also like to express my thanks to the following individuals: Joan Barker, John Colledge, Jenni Dobson, Pat Fox, Malcolm Hornsby, Squire de Lisle, Chris Mullins, Maureen Partridge, P. J. Rippin, Mark Sentance, Richard and Sue Smith, and Meg Williams.

BIBLIOGRAPHY

Bell, David. *Leicestershire and Rutland Murder Casebook.*
Countryside Books, 1995
Bell, David. *Leicestershire Ghosts and Legends.*
Countryside Books, 1992
Gravett, Christopher.*The Battle of Bosworth.* Osprey
Publishing, 1999
Green, Susan E. *Further Legends of Leicestershire and
Rutland.* Leicester Research Dept, 1985
Green, Susan E. *Selected Tales of Leicestershire.* Leicester
Research Services, 1971
Hornsby, Malcolm. *The Loughborough Job.* Dave Dover,
(reprint) 1998
Lamb, V.B. *The Betrayal of Richard III.* Research
Publishing Co, 1959
Meadows, Jack. *Leicestershire – some legends and stories.*
1996
Page, Nick. *Lord Minimus.* HarperCollins, 2002
Pipe, Marian. *Tales of Old Leicestershire.* Countryside
Books, 1991
Potter, Jeremy. *Good King Richard?* Constable, 1983
Potter, T. R. *History and Antiquities of Charnwood Forest.*
Hamilton, Adams & Co, 1842
Tanner, Michael. *Crime and Punishment in Victorian
Leicestershire.* Anderson, 1981
Williams, D. T. *The Battle of Bosworth Field.* Bosworth
Publications, 1973
Williams, Meg. *Holywell – from Hermitage to Research
Centre.* Gas Centre Research Centre, 1993